"I was impressed with Matt Mielnick's unique insight into my son's sensory issues and his ability to communicate that information in non-clinical language."

—*Angela Bankson, Parent*

"Recognizing that there are rarely simple answers to explain complex issues, Matt Mielnick strives to give us something to work with by explaining the brain–body relationship and taking us on a tour of the sensory system so we can begin to grasp the method to the madness at hand, recognize the stress it places not only on the child but the family as a whole, and begin to put strategies in place to help the child increase their availability for learning and more adaptively interact with their environment."

—*Michele Kohler LCSW, Evaluation Unit Supervisor at New York League for Early Learning*

UNDERSTANDING SENSORY PROCESSING DISORDERS IN CHILDREN

A Guide for Parents and Professionals

Matt Mielnick

Jessica Kingsley *Publishers*
London and Philadelphia

First published in 2017
by Jessica Kingsley Publishers
73 Collier Street
London N1 9BE, UK
and
400 Market Street, Suite 400
Philadelphia, PA 19106, USA

www.jkp.com

Library of Congress Cataloging in Publication Data
Title: Understanding sensory processing disorders in children / Matt Mielnick.
Description: London ; Philadelphia : Jessica Kingsley Publishers, [2017] |
   Includes bibliographical references and index.
Identifiers: LCCN 2016053037 | ISBN 9781785927522 (alk. paper)
Subjects: | MESH: Sensation Disorders--physiopathology | Sensory
   Thresholds--physiology | Child
Classification: LCC RJ486 | NLM WL 710 | DDC 618.92/806--dc23 LC record available at
https://lccn.loc.gov/2016053037

British Library Cataloguing in Publication Data
A CIP catalogue record for this book is available from the British Library

ISBN 978 1 78592 752 2
eISBN 978 1 78450 568 4

Printed and bound in the United States

ACKNOWLEDGMENT

Nearly 50 years have passed since Occupational Therapist A. Jean Ayres first offered her remarkable, eye-opening theories referred to as Sensory Integration, or more recently Sensory Processing. This model offered an illuminating new perspective from which to consider those invisible influences that contribute to some children having significant problem behaviors and/or learning difficulties. No longer were the worlds of science and education forced to squeeze these children into the neat categories of medical, developmental, neurological, or psychological dysfunction that were professionally available at the time, but often missed the mark in terms of both diagnoses and treatment. Her work and the discussions it sired represent a global shift in what we know about ourselves, and more specifically, how to make legitimate help available to the children we love so much. This short work, out of concern for the volumes of sophisticated discussions that have followed since then, attempts to offer a plain-language explanation for the world that Ayres's profound insights opened up for parents and educators.

CONTENTS

Preface   9

1. Introduction to the Sensory System   11
How it's supposed to work   15
The sensory continuum   20
A note on differences   22

2. Sensory Thresholds   24
The high threshold/poor registration child   27
The under-responsive child   33
   Carl   35
The sensory seeker   44
Body awareness issues   48
   Ilya and Alex   50
The low threshold/highly responsive child   69
The sensory sensitive child   70
   Tyrone   72
The sensory averse child   80
   Scott, Peyton, and Neal   87
   Whit   114
The self-regulation piece and
both ends of the continuum   123

3. A Cautionary Tale...   **127**

4. Finally...   **131**
   Special acknowledgment   135

   An OT's Suggestions for the Pre-school Classroom   137
     Fine motor   138
     Writing problems and practice suggestions   138
     Cutting difficulties   142
     Sensory kids   143
     Movement options   151

   Index   155

PREFACE

This is a little book. From the moment I decided to write it my objectives were clear: Present an explanation of Sensory Processing Disorder in language that was as clear to a parent or a new student as it was to a professional, without being condescending...and then get out of the way! For sure, there are many informative, often scholarly works on this topic that require a considerable amount of time and study before you can begin to understand their complex ideas, and yet, the material is so compelling that its focused reading audience is willing to commit considerable effort in their determination to raise their level of understanding. If they are students or experienced professionals then their preliminary studies have already prepared them for the level and vocabulary of the discourse. What a different experience this describes than that of a distraught parent of a child with atypical behaviors, desperate for an explanation, and often faulting themselves for not fully understanding the science and medicine described in primary texts and in the professional reports written about their child.

I have a different story to tell. I have evaluated over a thousand young children as part of the process of determining their eligibility to receive occupational therapy services through Early Intervention and Preschool entitlement programs. As part of each of these evaluations I routinely take the time to explain to parents how I understand our sensory system to work, and how inefficiencies in key parts of this system can have profound impacts on a child's behaviors. I have tried to consistently use direct, down-to-earth language, as well as easy-to-relate-to examples and metaphors. When my explanation inevitably collides with those big three-hundred-dollar technical words, I do my best to define them and explain how they might be relevant to the problems their child is reportedly experiencing.

Here's the part that's most gratifying. At the conclusion of these discussions the parent often has a sheen of recognition on their face. Many times I've been told that my explanation made sense for the first time, and that they were able to recognize their child in one or more of the various sensory descriptions I offered, even after their own efforts to research the subject and do the suggested readings about sensory processing had thwarted them.

As rewarding an experience as this is, it's also not uncommon to get a follow-up phone call within a day or two from that same parent. As compelling and clear as the explanation seemed to be at the time, they found it frustrating when they tried to communicate what I had said to them to their husband, other family members, or close friends. As such, they were perhaps somewhat better prepared to deal with their child's issues, but just as isolated as before. It reminds me of when I have a particularly lucid dream and the exhilaration it offers. But try as I might, I can't remember any of the details of that dream on the morning after.

This is my morning-after book.

CHAPTER 1

INTRODUCTION TO THE SENSORY SYSTEM

"You don't see things as they are. You see things as you are."
Talmud

I find it helpful to start with the most basic of questions: What do we know about this wondrous body we occupy? My explanation would go something like this: We all start off as the new product of a living seed and a living egg. This new microscopic entity, in most cases already quite hearty, quickly starts to develop according to a genetic plan, guided by the most basic instincts to survive and to reproduce. Within a few weeks, and then months, a network of discrete but highly integrated systems evolves to meet the demands of those instincts and perform the most basic of our bodily functions. A chain of digestive organs breaks down and conveys our food along a canal in which the altered product can be processed and used for its nutritional value. The respiratory system takes in essential gases from the atmosphere and captures them in our lungs until oxygen can be absorbed into the bloodstream, and other gases can be released outside of our body. The bloodstream then circulates through an extensive network of vessels, delivering the life-giving oxygen on a cellular level, pumped continuously by the mechanical workings of the heart. A waste management system claims the final products of digestion and eliminates unwanted solid and liquid wastes. Our muscles, bones, and connective elastic tissues form a hinged armature that enables us to meet truly impressive mobility challenges, covered and protected by a pliable but durable outer layer of skin. There's an electrical system of sorts that sends purposeful signals from our brain along a highway of nerves that animates these structures to run, walk, jump, dance, and shoot baskets.

And of course there's the brain. The brain sits in the governor's mansion and makes executive decisions about how all of these organs and organ systems should work together as we engage with the world on a moment-to-moment basis. It does so by interpreting information it receives about our environment via these nerve paths, and then offers a response, which is then sent to parts of our body to be acted upon. The staggering importance of the computer in today's world is a convenient and accurate metaphor for this amazing organ. The computer evaluates and processes inputted data, categorizes it, draws conclusions about how the data is relevant to its goals, and then issues directives to all of the component systems connected to it that serve at its command. But just as the computer requires someone to input the data that it needs to accomplish its impressive work, neither can the brain take all the credit for collecting information about the world we move through. For this it relies on another bodily system—an integrated partnership of antennae and receptors, all hooked up to the mainframe, and incessantly collecting and delivering information 24/7. Unlike the other physical systems mentioned above that tend to their specific duties discreetly inside our body, this other system is pointed outwards. It is our interface with the world, armed with a squad of investigators, reporters, and sentries. It is the keystroke on an otherwise blank document. And in order to accomplish its work, it enlists the entire surface area of our skin, our joints, our muscles, nerve pathways, and those fascinating facial features that other people most immediately recognize us by (after all, we're not just a bunch of pretty faces). It is nothing less than our body's ambassador to the world, a sensory system that moves us forward with rewards of pleasure and protects us with signals of caution— the same five senses that we first learn about in elementary school (plus a few other equally important, but curiously less celebrated, sense mechanisms).

It's interesting that we don't typically regard each of the individual sense "organs," and the magic they perform, as part of a highly sophisticated, integrated network that collects and processes the information for everything we know about our world. First, we tend to only give credit to those obvious external structures—we smell with our nose, see with our eyes, hear with our ears, taste with our tongue, and feel with our fingers—as though the process of each distinct sensory experience begins and ends with each of these body parts. Of course the truth of the matter is that these distinctive structures are only the hardware components, each acting basically as an antenna to collect this vital external information about our environment. The information must then be transmitted along specific neural pathways to the brain. The brain's job is then to identify and decode this information on a cellular level (make "sense" of it) and then generate an appropriate response.

We also tend to hold onto the assumption that our sensory system is designed primarily to heighten our pleasurable experience of the world—fragrant aromas, delicious tastes, velvety textures. No wonder some parents seem relieved when they learn that their children are dealing with a sensory issue rather than some more stigmatizing behavioral or psychological complaint. It's such a lovely area to spend time in!

Before we go any further, try to wrap your mind around the profound responsibilities that our sensory systems working together undertake for us, and the profound influence that this sensory activity can exert on our life. Think about it. We never really have an immediate, first-hand experience of the world we pass through. We do not actually experience the color green or the fragrance that a beautiful flower gives off. What we experience is the message that each of these sources sends out—a message that is collected by these sense organs, translated into neural code, and then transmitted to our highly individual brains to make sense of. Each message is simply a representation of that small piece of the world that you directly encounter, like a photograph or the mechanical product of a voice on a telephone. This is what it boils down to. We do not directly experience the world around us. We experience its messages. And if any of the components of this sensory system that we depend on to collect, transmit, and process these messages aren't operating efficiently, reliably, and accurately, then the messages we receive are also dubious, skewed, and incomplete (like the blurred photograph in a newspaper or the weak voice on a phone with a low battery). The consequences of not being able to rely on the accuracy of these messages can impact how we hold our bodies upright, how we move safely and confidently in the personal space we pass through, how comfortable (or threatened) we are as we come into contact with the events of our days, and how successfully we can attend to the priorities of our major life roles—family member, student, worker. The potential impact is nothing less than this. Weaknesses or defects in sensory processing can interfere with our typical ability to function in these roles as significantly as disease, injury, or disability.

HOW IT'S SUPPOSED TO WORK

When you think about it, everything we know about the world we live in starts with information we take in through our senses. After all, we are not enlightened beings, born with an elaborate pre-knowledge about our environment. We collect information about our immediate surroundings throughout our day, and even as we sleep, using those same senses that we learned about in the fourth grade. We receive visual information through our eyes. We first make sense of music, noise, and the spoken word using our ears. Our nose helps to alert us to something that smells fragrant or vile. The taste buds on our tongue are charged with the job of first sorting out when something tastes sweet or sour, salty or bitter. And for some reason, back in grade school (when we are first taught about our senses), our fingers got all the credit for our sense of touch. The more accurate statement of course is that the entire surface of our skin is covered with a number of different microscopic tactile sense organs, each type of receptor performing a very specialized and discriminating job. Certain organs just under the surface of the skin detect firm pressure, others respond to sharp pressure, still others to only light touch. There are still other skin receptors that relay temperature information, and even our sense of itch. Each one of these specialized tactile receptors is hooked up to the brain by way of specific, dedicated nerve pathways, like freight cars traveling on a certain train track that only carry a specific product like corn syrup or coal.

There are two other important sensory information systems that we generally don't hear about in grade school. The first one is our *vestibular* system. Most of us give ourselves some credit for knowing what our vestibular system does. We commonly refer to it as our sense of balance, and associate it with some function of the inner ear. It's obviously a little more involved than that. One of the primary responsibilities our vestibular sense has is to tell us when our head is held in an upright position. Think about it. Unless you're a car mechanic or a modern dancer, most of us go through our entire waking day with our head held in a vertical position. We are essentially erect beings, performing nearly all of our functional tasks with our eyes level, standing straight, all guided by having our head in a neutral position. The way this works is actually pretty impressive. Inside our inner ear is a small cup-like formation, partially filled with fluid. Located on the walls of this cup and protruding just over the surface of the fluid are hair-like structures that are actually sense receptors. When our head moves out of the vertical, the surface of the fluid remains level as this cup tilts. The fluid surface then comes in contact with these hairs, triggering a strong message to the brain that the head is no longer straight up and down. When this message is delivered and interpreted clearly we can then restore our head to a vertical position until the fluid is no longer brushing against these hairs and sending these potent signals. This simple mechanism has the enormous responsibility of telling our brain how to position our head in the upright position, a function that we depend on in order to carry out so many of our daily activities. Our vestibular mechanisms also tell us when we are moving, and distinguish whether that movement is along a straight path or more of a rotary path.

The final sensory system that we don't typically hear much about is our *proprioceptive* system. Proprioception is a fancy three-hundred-dollar word for our sense of "weight-bearing." When I stand up, gravity pulls the weight of my body towards the ground. In the process our bones are pushed together at those intersections where one bone meets another—the hinges of movement that we call joints. These joints are packed with specialized receptors—tiny physical cellular structures—that recognize when the bones are pushed together or pulled apart. Consider this. The only way you can stand up from your chair and walk with confidence to the nearby doorway is by having a "sense" of your weight on your hips and knees and ankles, unconscious as this sense might be most of the time. As you take a step and focus most of your weight on your forward leg you also relieve some of the pressure on your other leg as the bones relax and pull slightly apart at the involved joints. These forces acting on these receptors—pushing the bones together at the intersection of joints and relieving them of pressure as the bones slightly distract—are essential to our ability to plan and control our movements.

Consider what happens when your leg falls asleep. Any attempt at walking in a coordinated fashion across the room is thwarted. Your leg is numb—without "feeling." Your efforts to support your weight are hampered by your ankle giving way or your knees buckling. So, what is really happening here? It's not that your leg has some form of temporary paralysis, or that the blood flow has been interrupted. By sitting in an awkward position you have actually crimped those nerves that connect these joint receptors to the brain along sensory pathways. Thus, the messages that normally alert you as to when you have placed your weight on your legs or feet have been compromised temporarily. For the time being your brain does not efficiently register where these extremities are, and cannot send the appropriate commands to move them in your usual coordinated fashion. In other words, you simply do not "feel" your leg, or more accurately, the feeling in your leg does not fully register in your brain. Imagine what it would be like if this line of communication did not work efficiently a good deal of the time.

You need to feel your body weight and the effects of gravity in order to plan and execute coordinated, confident movements. And when you can't feel this reassuring sense of weight-bearing, you may think of little else until that feeling is restored, in much the same way that you stop what you're doing to stomp your foot on the ground to restore feeling when it has fallen asleep. Keep that response in mind, for it is potentially very telling with regards to certain sensory children that we will discuss later.

Our proprioceptive sense is one of the primary mechanisms we have for how we feel our body. It enables us to move without deliberating on whether our legs will support us. It tells us where our body parts are without looking at them, allowing us to coordinate and target the movements of our extremities as we undertake a task. Essentially it is our means of experiencing resistance and pressure, without which we could neither perform work nor recognize reasonable movement ranges that keep us safe from harm.

How all these sensory networks work is actually quite impressive. These vigilant sensory receptors operate every second of the day to collect specific information from the external world. This information is then somehow translated into a neural code—an intelligent signal representing the sensory experience—which is then transmitted along nerves to the brain. If this signal is conveyed efficiently and the proper neurochemical reactions occur, then the brain can acknowledge the information and formulate a response. "That light is too bright, so I should shield my eyes," or "I don't like the way that sand feels on my bare feet, so I'll put on my sandals," or "The stove is too hot, so I'll keep my distance." The whole gamut of comfort/pleasure, caution/pain, the sum of our experience, is acknowledged by the brain's ability to efficiently process this sensory input. But, this raises a central question. It's fairly obvious that every single one of us is distinct and different from everyone else, even within members of the same family. I'm referring not just to appearance, but also to the way in which our various physical systems (and brains) are constructed, and how well these various bodily systems do their respective jobs. What happens—depending on these physical differences with regards to these specific sensory pathways—if some specific sensory information (auditory, visual, tactile, vestibular, proprioceptive) en route to the brain is compromised because the physical/neurochemical process is either inefficient or, for that matter, hyper-efficient?

THE SENSORY CONTINUUM

Most of us are able to proceed through this step-by-step process fairly well. We collect information about the world around us. We translate the information into intelligent signals and then transmit those along specific nerve paths leading to the brain. The brain processes the information and issues an appropriate command for our body to react.

When things are working well we are also able to depend on a few other sensory mechanisms that allow us to perform the functions of our day-to-day lives. First, our brain is normally able to sort through this constant stream of sensory input and prioritize what is new and important. In other words, it is able to tune out most of what is redundant around us. What would our life be like if we had to attend to every siren on the street, every blinking light, or the slightly rough surface of our coffee mug each time we raised it to our lips, as though they always seemed like new experiences and central to our affairs? The brain knows how to habituate to these familiar sensory events—that is to say, it knows how to tune them out or suppress them. Obviously, while the brain is able to limit which sensory events we need to respond to, it also is able to make decisions to allow other sensory information to register based on its importance and intensity. These two mechanisms—of inhibiting some sensory messages and facilitating others—are extremely important parts of the sensory process.

The final important step in this sensory process has to do with the brain's need to come up with a response to a trigger event that is appropriate. This is the self-regulation piece that you've likely heard about so much. Think about it. We are constantly met with extreme sensory challenges from our immediate environment. We live in a world where sweltering summer temperatures can rise above 100 degrees, only to plummet to well below zero in some places during the winter. And yet most of us put our pants on in the morning, jump in the car, and go to work for seven or eight hours under these taxing conditions. These are sensory extremes. Yet somehow our brain is able to accommodate to them and deal with them in a way that enables us to function. Children must also be able to respond to their sensory environment with a timely, measured, and appropriate response if they are going to be able to function, even in the most docile environment. Unfortunately, for some children, even the most benign sensory challenges result in a dramatic and unregulated response.

These sense mechanisms, all connected to the supercomputer of our brain, are what we rely on to plan, guide, and protect our bodies as they negotiate with our constantly shifting environment. When all of these systems work efficiently on a physiological level, then we give very little conscious thought to how smoothly these important processes take place—no more than our awareness of each breath we take or each time our heart pumps. But if some part of the sensory network does not work optimally, then a person can feel unsure, confused, or threatened, and most likely will be faced with significant challenges.

If you were to plot the efficiency of these sensory networks on a linear scale—a continuum—then the majority of us would occupy a large section in the middle of this scale, in what we can refer to as a comfort zone. To be sure, most of us who can identify themselves in that comfort zone may have some kind of atypical response to certain stimuli. For example, I cannot walk barefoot on a gravel driveway or on a beach. But the great majority of us are able to adjust to these peculiarities and continue to function without having to focus most of our resolve to overcome the discomfort. However, there are some children—let's talk in terms of children from this point on—who struggle with some part of collecting, transmitting, or processing this sensory input, or regulating a response to this information. These children would fall outside of this comfort zone at one end or the other.

Our discussion of which end of this continuum they should be plotted on has to do with how difficult it is, or how sensitive they are, to meeting chemical "thresholds" in the brain. For now it is enough to point out that these extreme processing disorders at either end of our graph involve more than just an aversion to tooth brushing or walking barefoot. It is safe to say that almost everyone has some sensory discomfort of one kind or another. However, sensory processing in children is identified as a serious problem when its characteristic behaviors persistently impact on or impede learning, socialization, and/or appropriate behaviors.

A NOTE ON DIFFERENCES

In a world filled with billions upon billions of people, one of the few things we can state with certainty is that none of us are exactly alike, an amazing reality pressed home strikingly each time we recognize that no two faces are exactly the same. We each have our physical strengths and our physical shortcomings—strong heart/weak kidneys; bad knees/ dexterous fingers. The multiplicity of our species, the genetic predispositions of our parents, the early life experiences and traumas that we contend with—all contribute something to the unique physical blueprint that we individually become.

We may draw upon all of these influences, but the end product is entirely our own.

Even within families, I am always impressed with the stories I'm told of how different one child is from another. It reinforces my conviction that these differences are to be respected first and foremost when assessing a child's sensory status, for these special differences play an essential part in shaping their future. As such, I am always cautious when a parent tells me that "the apple doesn't fall far from the tree," or "I was just like that when I was a kid, and look how well I turned out." We may very well inherit some of our parents' fortitude, strengths, and inclinations. But our struggles and weaknesses are all our own. The height of the bar that we all have to jump over to lead a comfortable and productive life is different for all of us.

To bring this back to the discussion of our sensory status, we are all "wired differently." These differences represent nothing less than our ability to adequately confront life's many difficulties, often found in the most routine and unexpected encounters. What is easy for one child can be painfully difficult for another. No parent can reasonably insist that they know what their child is fully experiencing, as similar as their stories may be. The summits that a parent has crossed may be insurmountable for a son or daughter whose sensory systems are differently equipped. Each of us, from a sensory perspective, needs to be viewed as one of these unique marvels of nature, with our many unique strengths and weaknesses located somewhere along our personal continuum. To ignore these essential differences runs the risk of throwing your child into deep water based on your own ability to swim safely to shore.

CHAPTER 2

SENSORY THRESHOLDS

If we are in fact all "wired differently," how can we begin to describe and better understand these complex physiological differences in our sensory mechanisms? Or to put it differently, why are some children so terribly sensitive to aspects of their environment, while others seem unperturbed by even profound sensory events quite near to them? In order to proceed, we first need to add another term to the discussion— "threshold." A threshold is another one of those terms that we think we understand. Most of us think of a threshold as a line, perhaps beneath a doorway, that indicates you have entered a new space once you have crossed it (for example, the groom carries the bride over the threshold). In the vernacular of the brain, the word "threshold" has a more specific meaning. A threshold is that point in the sensory process (in the brain) at which a behavioral response to a stimulus is generated. In sensory terms, when the neurochemical processes that convey specific sensory messages along the nervous system to the brain register sufficiently for the brain to recognize the signal and then send a command to react, then the threshold is met. It is that point at which our arousal system is activated. It is that exact moment when sufficient neurochemicals have been exchanged in a cellular reaction to alert us to the sensory event we have just experienced.

Take the example of a set of balance scales. On one plate you may have an ounce of sand. Now summon the patience to add one grain of sand at a time to the empty plate. At first nothing happens, even after adding grain after grain. That point at which one additional grain of sand causes the scale to tip is the point at which you've met its threshold—the point at which you've generated a response (yes, a threshold is often called a "tipping point"). Let's consider what the implications are of having to add either very little sensory input or a profound amount of it, in order to reach such a threshold and generate a functional response.

In our brain we may have high sensory thresholds, and/or low sensory thresholds. High thresholds are difficult to achieve. In the example of the scales, a big pile of sand on the first plate would require a considerable amount of sand to be added to the empty plate before causing the first plate to lift. To restate this in the context of our sensory discussion, a high neurological threshold would require considerably more sensory input of some kind—light, sound, touch, motion, pressure—before the brain could fully appreciate that input enough to respond to it.

Conversely, low thresholds, as you would expect, are quite easy to achieve. Such low sensory thresholds in the brain are therefore achieved with relatively little input. Although this sounds like a particularly efficient and therefore helpful scenario, it needn't be. Because low thresholds are met so easily, they are also achieved much more frequently, insisting that your brain must attend to the event each and every time. It is also likely that the intensity of the Low Threshold child's reaction to a sensory event is also much more dramatic. In other words, a neurochemical message conveying even routine sensory input not only easily meets such a low threshold, but also may overwhelm the process as well. The process of meeting these easy, frequent thresholds can therefore be quite uncomfortable or even distressing.

Each of us has a uniquely different threshold for each of our sensory pathways, since each sensory message travels along its own dedicated route to the brain. Light follows one nerve path, temperature another, firm pressure still another, and so on. We may react quite differently to sound than we do to touch. For example, we may recoil dramatically from even slightly elevated lighting levels, while we are also able to walk barefoot on a rocky beach without registering any pain or discomfort. Most of us are familiar with our own unique sensory experiences that we consistently find challenging (and most of us have one or more of these idiosyncrasies). Fortunately, for most of us, these atypical responses do not interfere with our life to the point where we can't function. For some children, however, the point at which these responses are generated—the point at which these thresholds are met— can profoundly impact on their play and their work.

Some children display a pattern of behaviors that is classically consistent with high threshold types of responses. In other words, they may have a similarly characteristic response to a range of different sensory triggers. The child who is under-responsive to sound may also appear under-responsive to light and touch, as well as proprioceptive and vestibular input. Other children consistently demonstrate equally pervasive across-the-board responses to a low threshold condition. The child who vehemently protests getting their hands icky with finger-paints may also tantrum in response to volume levels at a concert attended by many other more tolerant children, giving the impression of a truly hypersensitive child.

On occasion, a child may exhibit both high and low threshold responses at a dramatic level. We'll save that discussion for later.

All of this brings us to the core of our discussion, as expressed in the following question: What are the real-life consequences of these high threshold and low threshold reactions in the brain? What types of behaviors does the High Threshold child consistently engage in? What are the behavioral manifestations of a child with unusually easy-to-achieve low sensory thresholds? We'll discuss each of these conditions separately in the following sections.

THE HIGH THRESHOLD/POOR REGISTRATION CHILD

I'm about to board a train for a trip that is absolutely necessary, but couldn't come at a more inopportune time. For days now I've been waiting for an important call from someone with information critical to my career. As I get on the train I semi-consciously feel for the cell phone in my coat pocket. The train leaves on time, and I start to doze. Not too far into the trip, just as the train passes through the first of a series of tunnels, and valleys lined with high cliff faces, I hear a faint, gargled noise that I find fairly easy to ignore, until my neighbor across the aisle taps me on the shoulder to tell me my phone is ringing. It's not the robust, familiar ringtone from Beethoven's Fifth, but a throaty, interrupted, and barely recognizable version, obviously impacted by the poor reception along this corridor. I put it to my ear and say hello, but the only thing I can clearly understand from the other party is the name of the person I've been so anxious to hear from. Bits of garbled speech follow, but I can't understand most of what is being said to me. I start asking the obvious cell phone question—"Can you hear me?"—calmly at first and then more and more vociferously, until I start raising attention to myself among the other passengers. This information is simply too important, and I need it now. I start to squeeze the phone with both hands, and reach the point where I'm practically yelling into it, as though this will somehow improve the reception, until the connection is lost. My attempts at returning the call are equally unsuccessful, and my preoccupation with this process is all consuming, even to the point where I do not recognize that the conductor is now towering over me with his arms folded, waiting to admonish me for these inappropriate behaviors.

This is why this analogy is so compelling for me: The phone connection is obviously the sensory pathway that delivers essential information to a child about their immediate environment. Even though there is nothing mechanically wrong with the instrument, this period of poor reception results in important information being received that is somewhat familiar and identifiable, but largely unavailable. At first the traveler, in his languorous state, essentially ignores the pathetic, wimpy sound of his ringing phone. How could it possibly be important? When the traveler finally recognizes the source and importance of this information, the message is so incomplete as to be extremely frustrating. He then reaches a point where he is so exasperated and so intent on demanding more of the situation that he makes bold, obtrusive, and inappropriate choices around the other travelers on the train. This man is not deranged or someone who consistently makes such a spectacle, but his preoccupation and frustration over not receiving a strong, clear signal drive him to a state that he cannot control. Ironically, it is not the critical information he has missed that becomes so consuming, but rather the mechanical shortcoming of the communication device in this situation. Getting the phone to work efficiently again becomes his number one priority. In the process he loses all perspective of what is socially expected of him as a passenger surrounded by others.

The behavioral responses of the High Threshold child are similarly motivated by such an unsatisfying signal. They often reach the point where they try to find ways to add more profound input as a way of compensating for such a weakened and unsatisfying stimulus, often going overboard in the attempt.

The High Threshold child always reminds me of an old carnival game. Some of you have played this game at the state fair or at the traveling carnival that used to visit your town every summer. Others may have only seen pictures of it. In the game, a barker takes your money and hands you a heavy sledge hammer. He then invites you to pound on a large button resting on the ground with the hammer as hard as you can. This in turn sends a metal clanger up a tall metal column. At the top of this column there is a large bell fixed to the structure. If you can hit the button hard enough, you can ring the bell and win a stuffed animal. Obviously, on the midway the odds are staked against your winning. Not everyone can hit the button with enough force to ring that bell. Some watch as the clanger gets really close to the bell, only to see it reach its apogee short of the mark, and then fall silently back down to the ground. For certain individuals, ringing that bell consumes them, and their repeated failures to do so can get quite frustrating, perhaps to the point where they can think of nothing else, spend all their money trying, and ignore their girlfriend's urging to quit and go to the Ferris wheel—the only thing they want is to hear the sound of that bell. For the time being it is their only priority. It should be so simple, and how did that other little guy holding that stuffed panda do it?

The High Threshold child can be faced with a similar scenario. Obviously, ringing the bell is a metaphor for meeting a specific sensory threshold. The High Threshold child is faced with one or more difficult-to-achieve sensory thresholds (proprioceptive, vestibular, auditory, etc.). It is only after this threshold is met that the sensory event sufficiently registers to evoke an appropriate response. In other words, this child cannot fully appreciate some of the sensory experiences that convey important information about their world to them because it is difficult to meet the sensory threshold that allows the event to register in the brain. The process can be frustrating, or at the very least preoccupying. Once again, this could be specific to their auditory responses to their world, to their visual responses, their tactile, vestibular, or proprioceptive responses—or to a combination of varied sensory responses. Keep in mind these deficits are processing difficulties. There is nothing wrong with the mechanical attributes that contribute to visual or auditory acuity. Nor does this describe a neurological condition in which tactile sensitivity is impaired.

There's an old descriptive term that people used to use when speaking about one of the children in their extended family (or about one of the adults, for that matter) who fit this profile. One almost never hears it used anymore. People used to speak about children with "dulled senses." I honestly haven't heard it used in years and you may have never heard it spoken. But when you are trying to characterize the experience of the High Threshold child, this deserves a closer consideration. A word of caution is called for, however. The child who is referred to in this manner is not being identified as intellectually delayed. Instead, the term means just what it says. For some reason, such a person is consistently not registering some kind of sensory input to the degree that we normally recognize as immediate and convincing. Obviously, they are likely registering the experience to some extent, but this is one of those "find yourself somewhere on the continuum" issues. The experience is simply quite different, and generally not very satisfying.

Let's take the example of "pain." We think of external pain as arresting, intense (that's why we call it pain), and undeterrable. Pain is in fact an extremely important type of sensory tactile awareness. The experience of pain teaches us how and when to recognize safety limits. When something is initially painful, we back off and hopefully recognize the trigger events that are potentially harmful, so that we can avoid them in the future. We tend to take for granted that everyone reacts to pain in pretty much the same way. However, quite frequently, I have parents tell me that their son or daughter doesn't typically seem to register pain. They bounce back quickly from even significant falls, bumps, and bruises, or may not even have a visible reaction to vaccinations. (*Please note*: For that small group of parents who are reading this who see this type of response as a sign of their child's bravery or toughness, please return this book for a full refund—you just don't get it!) But the inability of a child to adequately register pain represents a very threatening situation. The child who cannot fully appreciate what such a red flag means—especially at a young developmental stage when safety limits cannot be easily identified through reason—may recognize few or be confused by limits at school, on the playground, on stairways, around appliances, and so on. This is the perfect example of the child with a "dulled sense" of their tactile world. Their information about their immediate world is diminished and incomplete, and the possible consequences are significant. These children are not impervious to feeling. They just have a difficult time fully processing the sensory event because of these steep neurochemical thresholds that we've started to discuss above.

It is important to keep in mind that as fascinating as all this brain science is, what really concerns parents and educators are the behaviors that result. No one actively worries about how difficult it is for their son or daughter to efficiently achieve neurochemical thresholds. They worry about Johnny's ignoring behaviors, or Debbie's seemingly deliberate crashing into walls, or Bennie's well-deserved reputation as a risk taker. Remember that sensory processing issues become a concern when consistent patterns of strongly atypical behaviors are identified. Patterns of behaviors are the most telling aspect of sensory evaluation. After all, there is no blood test for Sensory Processing Disorder.

So, just what are some of the significant behaviors that this inadequate registration of specific sensory input prompts the High Threshold child to engage in? After making a list of behaviors that I associate with the High Threshold child, I realized that they can be loosely arranged for discussion into three different categories. In one scenario—we'll call this the Under-Responsive child—the child's brain passively acquiesces to the difficulties of meeting these thresholds and simply accepts the consequences of not fully experiencing these external stimuli that routinely impact on them. In another—the Sensory Seeker—the child is motivated to actively compensate for this discomforting, inadequate processing of information by seeking out strong, additional sensory input. And finally, we have the child who is faced with body awareness challenges, a behavior set that describes what happens when a child has a diminished "sense" of where their body parts are in relation to the space they pass through.

THE UNDER-RESPONSIVE CHILD

The Under-Responsive child quite simply summons very little effort to further facilitate meeting those specific thresholds that are challenging for them, and passively accepts these conditions. It's as though some power shortage has imposed a brown-out. This Poor Registration child therefore often presents as a child whose arousal/alert system is not fully activated (because incoming sensory input has not reached those thresholds for response). Such a child may not adequately and efficiently register typical stimuli in their environment, and as a result may seem somewhat disengaged at times (thus explaining an important distinction between the child who doesn't participate in a group activity because they can't sit still through it, and the Under-Responsive child who drifts in and out of focus and centers on more preferential activities). The child is often quite sedentary, not properly motivated to physically engage with their world. As such, it is not unusual for this child to present with floppy postures, weakness, or poor stamina. This child may present with a very flat affect, with little of the animated and changing facial expressions we normally attribute to children. Their emotional range may also seem quite shallow.

Quite frequently, some of these children are very slow in responding to prompts, at times reaching the point where they seem to virtually ignore familiar and even emphatic auditory cues. In many cases like this parents have already followed up on these behaviors by having their child formally tested for a hearing dysfunction, only to find that there is nothing wrong with the mechanics of hearing. These children may not establish eye contact easily or may not readily pick up on other people's facial expression or body language. In some cases they are unaffected by having their hands or face messy after eating or play, and do not always protest or appear uncomfortable if their diaper is soiled or wet. In extreme cases, even typically painful trigger events do not ruffle them. These are the children who either appear unfazed by bumps and falls or vaccinations, or bounce back extremely quickly to resume the same risky behaviors that led to their mishap. In general, their sensory switch is not fully in the "on" position.

CARL

(An Under-Responsive child)

OCCUPATIONAL THERAPY EVALUATION

Name: Carl

Chronological Age: 3 yrs., 11 mos. (47 mos.)

Reason for Referral: Carl is being evaluated to assess sensory-motor functioning and to assist with future educational planning. Specific concerns cited have focused on possible sensory processing issues. Carl reportedly is very easily distracted, has a short attention span, and becomes easily overstimulated. Concerns were also noted that he has a poor sense of his body as it moves through the space he occupies.

This occupational therapy evaluation will formally evaluate fine motor and visual-motor abilities (grasp, manipulation of small objects, use of both hands, motor planning and execution, body awareness, eye–hand coordination) as they impact on pre-academic learning readiness and self-care routines; as well as consider whether there are sensory registration, processing, or regulation difficulties responsible for considerable discomfort, or behaviors that interfere with typical developmental gains or school preparedness.

Site of Evaluation: This mid-morning evaluation took place at Carl's preschool. I observed Carl during a group movement and dance activity and during his lunch. Fine motor testing was administered in a room provided by the school on the same floor as his class. The space was quite suitable in terms of spaciousness, cleanliness, and relative lack of distraction. I spoke with his mother by phone several days after my visit. I also spoke with Carl's teacher, as well as with an Early Childhood Program Supervisor who worked with Carl this past summer.

Birth/Medical History: Carl is the only child of Mr. and Ms. C (the couple have been separated since Carl was 13 months of age). Carl lives with his mother and sees his father on weekends. Ms. C reports that her pregnancy was unremarkable following a good course of pre-natal care. Carl was born full term via cesarean delivery when the labor would not progress. He weighed 9 lbs., 1 oz. Carl came home from the hospital with his mother. He has not been troubled by any persistent digestive difficulties, ongoing respiratory difficulties, or chronic ear infections. There have been no subsequent hospitalizations, serious illnesses, or injuries. Hearing and visual acuity reportedly raise no concern. He is currently in good health.

Background/Behavioral Observation: Ms. C remarked that she is "impressed" with her son's social skills. He approaches children appropriately at the playground and invites them to play. He visits the playground almost daily. Ms. C commented that he is very active during his play there and is competent on the various apparatus (although he is not a huge fan of the swing). She further remarked that he can be a "thrill seeker," and has "no sense of safety limits." Carl also has playdates at home approximately every other week. In terms of self-care Carl reportedly can feed himself using a fork and spoon. He eats a variety of foods. Ms. C described him as a "grazer" in that he eats small amounts throughout the day. He is cooperative with dressing, but still finds it difficult pushing his head through the opening in a shirt. He is toilet trained, although he continues to have toileting accidents (his mother commented that he is "not in touch with his own internal state").

Carl first attended the nursery school before he turned two years old. He remained in the program for approximately eight months, but Ms. C stated that he was not focusing on the class routines and activities. She removed him from the school and placed him under a nanny's care for the next several months. Carl started to attend the Y summer camp program in June of this year. Carl's teachers remarked that he often seemed disconnected from the class. They said that he seems unable to filter out unimportant stimuli and target an appropriate focus with his attention. This results in his becoming "overloaded," at times leading to his separating from an activity or having significant difficulty with regulating himself (there have been reported episodes of pushing, biting, and spitting). He can also be impulsive and grabby. As mentioned, concerns were also raised about his ability to navigate his body through space.

When I arrived Carl's class was engaged in a movement and dance lesson led by another teacher on a different floor. All 14 of his classmates were animatedly engaged in a game of "freeze," followed by some yoga poses and dancing. Carl, however, remained on the floor on the periphery of the group. His teacher mentioned that this was fairly typical of his behavior during such a class. She asked me if she should do what she could to facilitate his participation. I suggested that she give him some prompts, but to not press the issue with him. She approached Carl several times to invite him to join in, but he declined every time. Instead he variously leaned on the stack of floor mats, sprawled full-out on the floor, and placed his hands on and leaned against the full-length wall mirror. His body and hands seemed to be in constant, impressive contact with whatever surfaces were available to him. Eventually Carl lay down with his thumb in his mouth. At the end of the activity he rejoined his classmates in line and returned to the classroom without incident. The children then took out their lunch boxes and had lunch. Carl ate well and visited quietly with his neighbors. At one point he asked me to "please" help him take his straw out of the wrapper for his juice box. There were no behavioral over-reactions of any kind during my observation. As his classmates prepared for their rest period, Carl's teacher explained that he was to go with us to another room to play some games that I had brought. Carl did not seem apprehensive as we walked down the hall or when his teacher left us to return to the classroom. He was interested in the toys and task challenges I presented him with, and remained seated for the 25 minutes of activities without the need for a movement break. He did, however, seem to be scanning the room frequently and it was difficult at times for me to recapture his attention with verbal cues. Carl spoke in short phrases and simple sentences that were appropriate. He made reference to his mother with almost every statement that he made. He appeared to understand most of everything I said to him.

The **Peabody Developmental Motor Scales-2** is used to assess gross and fine motor skills in children from birth to six years old. The fine motor portion assesses grasp, hand-use, eye–hand coordination, and manual dexterity (the manipulation of small objects by use of the hands).

Fine Motor: Carl was able to pick up slender wooden toy candles and insert them into corresponding holes in a toy birthday cake using a neat pincer grip. He was able to pick up pennies one at a time from the table surface and place them through a coin slot. Carl was able to tower one-inch blocks ten-high, using good visual direction of his hand movements to neatly align the tower. With each of these one-handed targeting tasks Carl conspicuously held up his non-involved hand with his fingers tensed and curled (a fixing strategy used by some children to recruit other muscle groups as a way to compensate for an inadequate sense of stability in their trunk). He was able to remove and replace the top of a small screw-type jar. He was able to thread a lace through several large buttons and wooden beads, a task that requires each hand to perform a different part of a common task. He was able to replicate simple three-dimensional block designs. Carl held a crayon near the end of the shaft with a loose chuck-like grip and essentially dragged it along the paper resulting in marks that were barely discernible. At another point he resorted to holding it in a young, tight thumbs-up fisted grip that insists that his fingers, hand, and arm move as a fixed unit that does not allow for those independent movements of the wrist and fingers that are required for efficient drawing and writing practices. In this manner he was able to copy concise vertical and horizontal lines and a circle, but could not intersect the lines of an upright cross. He used an inefficient thumbs-down grip to cut paper. He independently cut through paper, but the effort was labored and extremely jagged.

Carl received a standard score of 4 (significantly more than 2 standard deviations below typical age-expected performance) on the grasping subtest (essentially due to his young, inefficient grip on the crayon and scissors) and a 7 (between 1 and 2 standard deviations below age-expected performance) on the visual-motor subtest of the Peabody. These scores represent a fine motor quotient of 73 indicating concerning delays in overall fine motor performance. It is further helpful to note that scores on the Peabody are based on the child's developmental ability to complete a task in any fashion, and not on the efficiency and quality of skill performance. Carl demonstrated associated hand movements with his non-involved hand, and tended to move his arm, hand, and fingers as a fixed unit during two-handed tasks. He relied on such strategies in an apparent attempt at stabilizing his hand movements. These suggest that the quality and efficiency of his fine motor performance is adversely impacted by a poor sense of stability in his trunk. This may be the result of diminished core muscle strength, but may also involve a poor sense of body awareness that does not give him adequate feedback to his hand while using a utensil (please see the following sensory section), leading him to respond with tensed strategies that are more convincing for him. Both theories represent potential deterrents to the quality and efficiency of fine motor attempts.

Sensory Integration: When professional evaluators look at how well a child's sensory systems are working, we are essentially looking at two main areas of potential difficulties, both of which can dramatically affect how a child behaves and matures developmentally. At one extreme is the child who requires an inordinate amount of some kind of sensory input before a sensory experience "registers" with them and allows them to react with an appropriate response. The other extreme describes children who are acutely sensitive to specific types of sensory experiences. Seemingly normal levels of sound, light, smell, oral experience, or touch may register with them as distracting, uncomfortable, or even distressing.

Based on his mother's responses on the Sensory Profile questionnaire, Carl achieved heightened scores (on the cusp between Probable Difference and Definite Difference score limits) for Low Registration-type behaviors. This refers to a High Threshold condition. A High Threshold profile describes a child's difficulty in efficiently registering certain types of sensory input because of high—and therefore difficult-to-achieve—neurological thresholds (a "threshold" in this context refers to that point at which enough sensory input has been processed in the brain to generate a response to the stimulus). A child who does not efficiently register various types of sensory input may be compelled to engage in exaggerated behaviors aimed at heightening the specific sensory input in an attempt to more convincingly register the experience in their body and restore some level of comfort.

Before discussing the particular actions and behaviors that result in such a score, it is perhaps helpful to explain how poor registration of sensory information might be specifically impacting on Carl's classroom performance. We typically consider sensory processing as the bodily system that allows us to collect, understand, and respond to external stimuli. Our senses of smell, taste, hearing, touch, and sight are all directed at the outside world. The information we collect about our external environment is essential in being able to safely adapt to and function in ever-changing situations. However, it must be recognized that some of our sensory systems have the responsibility of giving us vital information about our internal body as well. One example of this is the way that our vestibular systems give us a sense of movement, balance, and the level position of our eyes that we unconsciously depend on. Our proprioceptive sense gives us critical information about our experiences of pressure, resistance, and weight-bearing (our experience of gravity) without which we would not be capable of controlled movement and work. These senses have the essential responsibility of looking inwards and help us to make sense of motor planning and execution, safety limits, how to grade force, when there is too much food in our mouth, and when our bladder and bowels need to evacuate. Similar to the outward-directed senses, in order for these internal senses to work efficiently they need to be able to adequately discriminate between the constant barrage of internal signals that we must make sense of. The child who has a difficult time processing these internal signals subsequently doesn't readily know how to respond to these internal cues.

Now consider how Carl's mother and people in school have described him after observing and working with him. "Not in touch with his own internal state"; "unable to filter out extraneous stimuli"; "not at home in his own body"; "can't target with his attention"; "his sense of his body in space is horrid." These are strong statements that all essentially allude to this problem. The child who processes weak messages about his "sense" of his body is unable to effectively discriminate between stimuli, and in the process is not always able to recognize which signals are important and which ones are superfluous. Such a child is likely to pay as much attention to these superfluous signals, and in the process earns the label of being highly distractible and having poor attention. I believe this is what Carl is experiencing to some degree (certainly to the degree of generating concern among his caregivers). In partial response to his inefficient proprioceptive sense Carl reportedly seeks all kinds of movements that interfere with his learning opportunities. He also takes excessive risks during play (he's a "thrill-seeker") that compromise his safety. On less challenging notes, he doesn't notice when his hands and face are messy, and still has toileting accidents. Even my observation of how difficult it was to capture his attention with verbal cues from just a short distance away speaks directly to this. Despite no problems with his hearing acuity, Carl may simply not be filtering out auditory information that is potentially important. It is interesting to note that Carl's mother commented that he often feels guilty when he thinks he does something wrong. This kind of self-awareness may motivate him to distance himself from group physical activities that he knows he is challenged by.

Summary/Recommendations: Carl is a personable young boy who demonstrates good visual direction of his hand efforts, competent use of both hands to complete a common task, and a willingness to stay with an activity of interest. Fine motor scores are still concerning, and likely reflect the impact of not getting satisfying sensory feedback from utensils that he needs to control in the school environment, thus interfering with those automatic default grips that we expect to see in a child Carl's age. This further reflects on the difficulties he is reportedly experiencing in terms of motor planning and execution, sensory craving activities, and his wandering attention—all motivated by his poor registration of sensory signals.

I am therefore recommending occupational therapy services for Carl at this time.

THE SENSORY SEEKER

Children with behaviors consistent with a Sensory Seeking behavior pattern have a much more active and deliberate response to not fully meeting certain response thresholds in the brain. As we've discussed, it is only after such a high threshold is met that the sensory event convincingly "registers," and allows the child to fully appreciate the input. Children with this "high threshold" may not register in the same way the essential feedback through our muscles and joints that most of us take for granted in the simple acts of sitting or walking (remember those "proprioceptive" weight-bearing activities that we talked about). As such, they are unconsciously directed to seek out additional and enhanced opportunities for specific sensory input in hopes of satisfying these thresholds. Once again I find it helpful to use the analogy of having your foot fall asleep. For many people their immediate response when that happens is to stop whatever they're doing and stomp it forcefully and repeatedly on the floor. Such a dramatic response somehow facilitates restoring the feeling in your leg, only then allowing you to refocus on your normal activities. Likewise, the Sensory Seeking child may be continually faced with finding ways that somehow deliver a more convincing and settling sense of what they're feeling.

These children may appear very active continuously, constantly on the go, and compensate on their own by jumping, fidgeting, rolling, spinning, or climbing much of the time. They may at times deliberately crash into walls, objects, or other people. They may also be drawn to hang from bars on the playground (when the bones that meet at a joint are "distracted" or pulled apart by hanging on a bar, strong convincing signals are also sent to the brain from these joint receptors). Such actions all can potentially contribute firm pressure on joints which can help to amplify and compensate for dulled sensory messages.

Children who are Sensory Seekers also frequently have the reputation of being a thrill seeker or a risk taker because of their conspicuous pursuit of more dramatic input. These are the children who jump from the top of the stairway, or climb the slide ladder only to jump off the top platform. The promise of truly feeling the impact when they land is more motivating than weighing the possibly harmful consequences of such actions. In some situations these children somehow manage to convince their parents that the kiddie rides at the amusement park are not as much fun as the adult roller coaster, Ferris wheel, or bungee jump activities that they can enjoy over and over without any apparent fear or discomfort. These profound actions simply do not register fully with the High Threshold child, but oddly enough they are sufficiently powerful to help them feel something more genuine. It is appropriate to add that these children may not effectively register pain either.

Let's look at these behavioral presentations in a typical preschool classroom where many of these concerns are initially identified. The Sensory Seeking child typically can't sit still, and seeks out all kinds of movement activities to the point where they interfere with the typical routines and responsibilities of being a student. They are fidgety in line, and have difficulty participating in group activities that call for them to sit quietly, wait, or take turns. The number one concern I hear teachers voice is that little Jeremy will consistently get up off the rug during a circle time group activity and leave the group to move around the room and explore his favorite stations. When seated at an activity table, the student cannot sit still. They may wrap their legs around the chair legs. They may push down on their chair seat forcefully with extended arms, or stand at the table and push down on the table surface, more effectively forcing the arm bones together at key joints. Some children may choose to actually tall kneel on their chair seat (a position that many of us would find quite painful). In doing so a child focuses their body weight on as small a body surface area as possible, greatly accentuating the weight-bearing experience. This same interpretation can also help to explain why some children persistently walk on their toes (try either of these positions yourself to experience how heightened this feeling can be). One child I recently observed consistently stood in place with one foot pressed firmly on the instep of her other foot, and her arms tightly crossed, essentially with the same intention in mind. These are the children who quite often hate to wear shoes or socks, and prefer to walk barefoot, even when the surface is rough or irregular. Shoes simply get in the way between the child's bare feet and a truly distinct sensory opportunity such as walking on gravel.

The overall impression that this profile of behaviors helps to create is that the Sensory Seeking child's number one priority is to satisfy these sensory needs. This results in excessive movement and contact actions throughout their day, often to the point where they detach from their classmates and classroom activities (when they are actually in the process of vigilantly seeking out additional opportunities for movement and contact input that they feel they need). This is not the same as hyperactivity or an Attention Deficit Disorder (ADD) designation, although it is understandably easy to confuse the two. However, the child wrestling with

ADD is not as clearly goal motivated as they are from one activity to the next.

Here are some other behaviors that are often attributed to these little ones: These kids are frequently prop-driven. They may insist on having something in their hand constantly— not a security blanket, but rather a small car, train, or favorite small toy that they can apply pressure to. They may play with toys inappropriately, using them primarily to make noise with and bang them on a table surface. They also might frequently use their hands to play with food, and excessively splash during a bath. One little girl I recently spent time with was preoccupied with repeatedly pulling her knee socks forcefully up her legs until they were stretched to their limit. Then there are the kids who hug or lean against the walls as they pass through the halls, or touch everything in reach as they walk through an open space. They are frequently the wrestling fans who love firm pressure, rough-housing, and being sandwiched between cushions.

These are all sensory motivated actions, and they're not even the most socially frowned-on ones.

The Sensory Seeking child may show a persistent and unusual need to touch, rub, and lean on other people, often to the point of irritating others. They can also be overly affectionate with others, often hugging them too tightly. Then there are the truly unfortunate negative behaviors— hitting, kicking, pulling hair, and even biting. Obviously, not every child who hits and bites is struggling with a sensory registration deficit. But the interesting report that usually distinguishes these aggressive acts by a truly Sensory Seeking child is that the child is clearly not doing so out of any malevolence. Instead it seems that the child sees these actions as a rough style of play that they have identified as a way of realizing exaggerated input, although they are clearly unaware of the social consequences of their actions.

Here's one final note on inappropriate biting, or the child who is constantly putting non-food objects in their mouth. The powerful muscles of the jaw can send very convincing signals to the brain, exactly the kind of strong sensory input that a child with poor registration is determined to find. Likewise, the child who has a tendency to overstuff food into their mouth until their cheeks are puffed out is actually stretching, and thereby activating the muscles in the oral cavity, making an otherwise dulled experience much more convincing.

BODY AWARENESS ISSUES

It is also likely that these same High Threshold/Low Registration conditions that motivate a child to seek out additional input through their muscles and joints give them a less confident "sense" of their body position in the space they occupy, causing them to have problems planning and carrying out their movements (leading to reports of them being "awkward" or "clumsy"). Remember, we rely on our sense of weightedness to tell us where our extremities are without having to look at them. Thus, the child who has a diminished sense of the space they occupy may seem to bump into objects or doorways for no apparent reason, or may not know how to position their feet and legs when climbing on a jungle gym. Similarly, the child may have a poor sense of how to target something with their arm and hand movements. When a child stacks blocks, for example, they need to adequately feel the excursion of their arm through space in order to know when the hand holding the block is approaching its target, and then be able to further control the even finer movement adjustments that allow the block to be properly aligned on the tower without knocking it over.

This child may also have a poor sense of how much pressure they are actually applying with their arms and hands. This is the little boy who "doesn't know his own strength," and often hugs others too tightly because he cannot properly interpret the feedback that he receives when applying pressure. He may also not be getting the clear feedback through his arms, hands, and fingers that we rely on for a clear sense of how much force to use with a fine motor task. Such a child will frequently grip a crayon or pencil very tightly (giving his fingers a white-knuckled look as the blood leaves his hand). Drawing impressions may also be quite dark, and the points of pencils and crayons will frequently break off because of the excessive force the child uses without realizing it. Needless to say, this inordinate amount of pressure on the drawing utensil can often quickly result in hand fatigue, not to mention frustration or impatience with such important academic learning opportunities. All of these can contribute to drawing and writing difficulties.

The High Threshold child's diminished sense of where their body is may also lead to social difficulties. They can easily misjudge when they are standing too close in someone else's personal space, either face to face or when standing in line numerous times throughout the school day.

Consider how distracting and frustrating it might be on an ongoing basis for a child to focus so much of their energy on identifying sensory experiences that will help them meet these thresholds. As such, they are constantly scanning their immediate environment for enhanced movement and contact opportunities, and thus are frequently seen as being distractible or willful. Obviously, this has the potential to seriously interfere with appropriate attendance, socialization, and participation levels, especially once they have started their school career.

ILYA AND ALEX

(Sensory Seekers)

OCCUPATIONAL THERAPY EVALUATION

Name: Ilya

Chronological Age: 3 yrs., 11 mos. (47 mos.)

Reason for Referral: Ilya is receiving this occupational therapy evaluation at the recommendation of his preschool in order to assess sensory-motor functioning and assist in future planning. The referral follows a screening and recommendation from an occupational therapist who visited the school. Concerns focus on his heightened activity level, unregulated behaviors, and apparent difficulties recognizing behavioral limits with other children's bodies. He does not currently receive related services through the Committee on Preschool Special Education (CPSE) program.

This occupational therapy evaluation will formally evaluate fine motor and visual-motor abilities (grasp, manipulation of small objects, use of both hands, motor planning and execution, body awareness, eye–hand coordination) as they impact on pre-academic learning readiness and self-care routines; as well as consider whether there are sensory registration, processing, or regulation difficulties responsible for considerable discomfort, or behaviors that interfere with typical developmental gains or school preparedness.

Site of Evaluation: This afternoon evaluation was conducted at Ilya's preschool where he attends Monday through Friday from 1 p.m. until 4 p.m. I observed Ilya as he transitioned through a number of classroom activities, during a class parade through some of the other classrooms, on the outside playground, and during a free-choice play period. I spoke with his parents several days after my visit. Fine motor testing took place in the school library just down the hall from his classroom. The space was quite suitable for the evaluations given in terms of spaciousness, cleanliness, and lack of distraction.

Birth/Medical History: Ilya is the only child of Mr. and Mrs. I. Mrs. I reported that her pregnancy was unremarkable following a good course of pre-natal care. Ilya was born two weeks past his due date. He has not been bothered by chronic ear infections or ongoing digestive complaints. Hearing and vision reportedly raise no remarkable concerns. There have been no subsequent hospitalizations, serious illnesses, or injuries. He is currently in good health.

Background/Behavioral Observation: Mrs. I described her son as being a very easy baby. She mentioned that he is "passionate about playing with other kids." In terms of self-care skills Ilya can feed himself with utensils, but he does so "quite awkwardly" according to his mother. He strongly prefers to have his parents dress and undress him. He is fully toilet trained. Mrs. I indicated that his heightened need to have contact with people and objects in his immediate environment as a two-year-old was the reason for the family's initial concerns (please see the sensory section). He has occasional playdates with friends from the neighborhood and with the older children of his babysitter. This is his first year in a preschool program.

I arrived at the school as the children in Ilya's class were in another room being led in a lesson by a Movement Teacher. Ilya was smiling broadly and obviously enjoying the activity. However, within the first few minutes that I watched Ilya, he launched himself against another child and tackled him without warning or provocation. This occurred repeatedly (no fewer than four more times in the remaining ten minutes of the class), each time very suddenly, giving the teachers very little warning (Ilya's teacher commented that the other children are now quite wary of his behaviors). The other children appeared annoyed and looked to their teachers for assistance. Ilya was pulled away each time and spoken to about how inappropriate and possibly harmful this could be. He listened intently each time, but then seemed unable to resist each subsequent impulse to push the other children. His body remained in constant motion, even during the short transitions between the teacher's exercises and during the ones that required the children to remain in place. He often ran back and forth across the circle of children, making loud noises as he did so. At other times he would approach a neighbor and hug them unexpectedly. I watched as he approached another little boy and got very close to his face with his and asked in a loud voice, "What's your favorite thing to do?" Still another time he approached a child from behind and suddenly crawled between the child's legs. When he was not on his feet running, Ilya was on the carpet rolling around.

The class then transitioned back to the classroom, got their coats and walked to the school's rooftop playground. Ilya was very animated and ran around for a while, again pushing some children in what appeared to be his invitation for them to play with him. He then found the school wagon. Two other children got on the wagon, and Ilya seemed delighted to pull this rather heavy load. When it was someone else's turn to pull he ran to the back of the wagon and held onto the rear frame and tried to pull on it as it moved forward. Curiously, Ilya never paid much attention to the playground apparatus and never left the roof surface as he played. The children then returned to the classroom to prepare for the parade. The children were seated in a circle as they discussed how this would take place. Several times Ilya got up and walked over to other children to hug them (sometimes forcibly), but was quickly redirected and seemed happy to accept the invitation from one of the teachers to sit on her lap each time. Ilya did not impress me as trying to commit any of these physical actions deliberately. They seemed to occur spontaneously and with little warning. The class parade came next and went off without any incidents.

Ilya came willingly with his teacher and me to the nearby library space. He sat opposite me at the table and was immediately interested in the box of toys I showed him for the fine motor challenges. He waited patiently for each chance to play with a toy after I had demonstrated it and remained seated for the 25 minutes of activities without the need for a major movement break. He worked well from visual demonstration and clearly understood what each task expected of him. Ilya spoke in full sentences that clearly showed that he understood and used language appropriately. There were no behavioral over-reactions of any kind during my direct testing. Upon completion of the testing he returned to the classroom with me and joined his teacher at a table for a table-top activity during the free-choice period. His teacher had prepared me that this was a particularly difficult part of the school day routine for him. However, he remained seated and attentive for the next five minutes as she played with him and the other children at the table.

Ilya's teacher claimed that his demeanor and performance during my visit were representative of his typical conduct.

Gross Motor/Neuromotor Assessment: Active range of motion in all joints is within functional limits. There are no dysmorphic facial features. Arms and legs are proportionate and of equal lengths.

There was no observable evidence of tremor or involuntary rapid eye movement that would suggest neurological involvement.

Muscle tone appears somewhat low in Ilya's hands, extremities, and trunk (his muscles feel more flaccid than firm when they are challenged or when resistance is applied). My first assumption was that Ilya was a fairly strong child based on the degree of physicality of his behaviors in the classroom and on the rooftop. However, during the fine motor testing he consistently used one of his arms to prop himself up on the chair seat as he worked on a task, often to the point where he seemed reluctant to engage this propped hand in some two-handed tasks (such as anchoring the paper as he tried to draw with his other hand). Hand and finger movements were quite stiff, as were the tense grips he employed to hold and control manipulatives and utensils.

He was unable to jump with both feet together off the ground, but rather consistently led with one foot followed by the other in more of a gallop. He was unable to walk on his open hands and extended arms wheelbarrow style while supported at his knees right from the onset of his attempt. These are strong indications of diminished strength and stability in his torso and extremities, and may explain why I did not see him engage in any climbing or jumping activities at the playground (this is also consistent with his mother's comments).

Transition movements between lying down, sitting down, and standing postures were labored and not smooth. I would recommend a physical therapy evaluation if one has not already been scheduled as part of this comprehensive evaluation process.

The **Peabody Developmental Motor Scales-2** is used to assess gross and fine motor skills in children from birth to six years old. The fine motor portion assesses grasp, hand-use, eye–hand coordination, and manual dexterity (the manipulation of small objects by use of the hands).

Fine Motor: Ilya was able to pick up slender wooden toy candles and insert them into corresponding holes in a toy birthday cake, but did not engage his index finger in a neat pincer grip as he picked up each candle. He was able to pick up pennies one at a time off the table surface, but had considerable difficulty in correctly positioning his hand position to align with the orientation of the slot as I deliberately shifted it with each successive attempt (resulting in several attempts in which the coin just flattened against the surface of the bank). Ilya was able to stack one-inch blocks ten-high, but his hand efforts were not visually directed, resulting in a very precarious alignment of the tower. After considerable effort, he was able to thread a lace through different-sized buttons and beads and retrieve the string from the other side, a task that requires both hands to perform a different part of the same overall task. He removed the top from a screw-type jar. Ilya held onto a crayon with several shifting grips, but primarily with a tight thumbs-down (pronated) fisted grasp, and switched the hand he used to draw with several times. As mentioned, he did not readily anchor the paper with his disengaged hand because of his tendency to prop his extended arm on the seat of the chair through many of the activities. Crayon impressions were at times extremely heavy (at one point he started pounding on the paper with the crayon). He was able to approximate copying a concise vertical and horizontal line, but the lines were meandering and usually lapsed into a scribble. He was able to replicate a small closed-end circle and an intersecting cross. He deviated from a pre-drawn straight line several times by more than 1/2 inch when attempting to trace over it. He held scissors in an inefficient thumbs-down grasp and was able to cut into paper, but not through it or along a guide line drawn on the paper.

Ilya received a standard score of 5 (significantly more than 2 standard deviations below age-expected performance) on the visual-motor subtest and only a 4 (seriously more than 2 standard deviations) on the grasping subtest of the Peabody. These scores result in a cumulative fine motor quotient of 67 with performance registering at only the first percentile rank for his age (only 1 percent of children his age rank at this level or lower). These are concerning scores.

Ilya's awkward, tensed strategies reflect the effects of a diminished core strength. This was further evidenced by his reluctance to engage both hands in some tasks because of his need to prop himself up on his one extended arm. A child's torso muscles must be prepared and firm enough to provide a stable basis for independent extremity use. Until he makes improvements in further strengthening his core muscle groups, he will likely continue to approach fine motor tasks (and meet gross motor challenges) with the same limitations, even as these tasks become increasingly more complex and demanding. His level of achievement as well as his approach to tasks also appear to reflect a developmental delay in these functional areas, with his approach to testing reminiscent of a developmentally younger child.

Sensory Integration: When professional evaluators look at how well a child's sensory systems are working, we are essentially looking at two main areas of potential difficulties, both of which can dramatically affect how a child behaves and matures developmentally. At one extreme is the child who requires an inordinate amount of some kind of sensory input before a sensory experience "registers" with them and allows them to react with an appropriate response. The other extreme describes children who are acutely sensitive to specific types of sensory experiences. Seemingly normal levels of sound, light, smell, oral experience, or touch may register with them as distracting, uncomfortable, or even distressing.

Based on his parents' responses on the Sensory Profile questionnaire, Ilya received elevated scores (in the Definite Difference range) for a Sensory Seeking behavior profile (what is referred to as a High Threshold behavior set).

His teacher's responses are consistent with this category, but stand in contrast in that they reflect behaviors that are much more significant in terms of their intensity and frequency. A High Threshold profile refers to a child who needs considerably more emphatic sensory input of one kind or another in order to satisfy a high—and therefore difficult-to-achieve—neurochemical threshold in the brain (a "threshold" refers to the point at which a reaction in the brain generates a response to a stimulus on the part of a child). It is only after such a high threshold is met that the sensory event convincingly "registers," and allows the child to fully appreciate the input and settle into a more comfortable, organized state and a more reasonable activity pace. Such children are aware of this unsatisfying response to stimuli and are generally intent on compensating for this inefficiency. They are very active and constantly scanning their immediate environment for opportunities to more vigorously activate pressure and weight-bearing (proprioceptive) receptors in key weight-bearing joints (thus earning them the description of being "Sensory Seekers," as well as quite distractible). Children with this "high threshold" may not register in the same way the essential feedback through our muscles and joints that most of us take for granted in the simple acts of sitting or walking, and compensate on their own by finding ways to experience forceful contact with their environment, and in general moving their bodies in an effort to activate these pressure receptors in key joints.

Mr. and Mrs. I's responses point out the following persistent behaviors: Ilya frequently seeks all kinds of movement and becomes overly excitable during movement activities. He touches people and objects excessively.

He mouths objects frequently and deliberately smells objects. Ilya is constantly "on the go" and is overly affectionate with others. Mrs. I shared with me that his excessive physicality was really the reason why they became concerned initially when he was about two years old. During Mommy and Me classes as a younger child he would crawl over babies and grab at their faces. He would look for opportunities at the playground to deliberately crash into other children repeatedly. Mrs. I commented that these playground behaviors seemed to have improved over the last year and she was therefore somewhat surprised that the school was reporting these intense behaviors again. That being said, she added that social occasions that are not outside have been extremely difficult for Ilya to regulate himself, and made it necessary for the family to leave after just a short while. She stated that he has always shown a complete disregard for other people's personal space.

School staff report that Ilya is extremely fidgety (similar to my observations of him during testing) throughout the school day, and this behavior seems to escalate over the course of the afternoon. He starts to touch others around him, frequently hangs on people, and gets in very close to their personal space. He deliberately makes loud noises, and finds some way of using his body to heighten his physical contact with his environment (usually involving pushing against things or people, squeezing or hugging them, or pulling against objects). He also shows an unusual need to touch or grab objects, toys, and surfaces, and frequently seems to need something in his hand. Even his seemingly more aggressive behaviors—including crashing into children, hugging them forcibly, and a few biting incidents—catch him by surprise and appear to be directed by his need for physical experiences that involve applying pressure and making strong impact, although he is unfortunately unaware of how inappropriate these actions are.

Before closing this discussion, it is important to discuss any apparent discrepancy between the little boy at home and the one at school. Remember that both reports acknowledge that Ilya at times seems unregulated with his movement and activity levels. However, Mrs. I expressed some surprise when the school reported the extent of these behaviors. In all likelihood, with regards to both sets of reporters, observations are honest and reliable accounts of behaviors within each respective context. And there's the difference. Sensory behaviors emerge in response to sensory triggers. A classroom is awash with movement and contact opportunities. Ilya probably starts his day in school at a more reasonable activity pace (which is perhaps why the school recommended that I plan my visit more towards the end of his school day), that later deteriorates once he has been exposed to the broad menu of movement triggers in a classroom, as well as ample opportunities to indulge in his Sensory Seeking needs. His first movement opportunities of the school day act as a reminder or catalyst of the strategies available to him. The dynamic is remarkably different than in most typical homes. Even in the relatively short lifetime of a four-year-old, parents make all kinds of accommodations for their children in the home environment, often unconsciously. Lighting or volume levels may be adjusted. Routines are followed that taper off activities when it is called for. Even the size of the living space sets some limits on most children. Ultimately, there are far fewer trigger events in a family's apartment space than mostly anywhere else. These are not children whose activity levels are at a constant peak. These are children who have a characteristic response directly linked to sensory events, and find the last important piece in the sensory processing chain—self-regulation—most challenging.

Summary/Recommendations: Ilya is a bright, friendly, and active young boy being raised in a caring and supportive household. Scores on standardized fine motor testing reflect significant concerns (well over 2 standard deviations below age-expected performance) characterized by his tight-fisted, immature grasp and control of drawing and cutting instruments. Of more pressing concern, he convincingly presents with difficulties with impulsivity, Sensory Seeking behaviors, inappropriate social behaviors, and distractibility that pose serious challenges to his ability to perform his role as a student in a busy classroom. I am therefore strongly recommending that Ilya receive occupational therapy at the CPSE level to address sensory registration and self-regulation issues and the impact they have on fundamental fine motor practices and classroom conduct. Such services would be most appropriate in a setting that makes suspended equipment and movement opportunities available to him as he works with his therapist. Services should also provide an opportunity to implement a sensory diet designed by Ilya's therapist to provide him with regularly scheduled opportunities of additional, appropriate input throughout his day. Careful consideration should be given to other in-class support services that could be made available to him for the remainder of this year.

OCCUPATIONAL THERAPY EVALUATION

Name: Alex

Chronological Age: 3 yrs. (36 mos.)

Reason for Referral: Alex is receiving this occupational therapy evaluation to assess sensory-motor functioning and assist in future planning. Concerns focus on his heightened activity, and impulsive and sometimes aggressive behaviors. He does not currently receive related services of any kind.

This occupational therapy evaluation will formally evaluate fine motor and visual-motor abilities (grasp, manipulation of small objects, use of both hands, motor planning and execution, body awareness, eye–hand coordination) as they impact on pre-academic learning readiness and self-care routines; as well as consider whether there are sensory registration, processing, or regulation difficulties responsible for considerable discomfort, or behaviors that interfere with typical developmental gains or school preparedness.

Site of Evaluation: This afternoon evaluation was conducted in one of the evaluation rooms in the agency office suite. The space was quite suitable for the evaluation given in terms of spaciousness, cleanliness, and lack of distraction. Mrs. A accompanied her son and remained with him throughout the evaluation visit.

Birth/Medical History: Alex is the younger of Mr. and Mrs. A's two children (he has a four-year-old brother). Mrs. A reported that her pregnancy with Alex was unremarkable following a good course of pre-natal care. Alex contracted Respiratory Syncytial Virus at 11 months of age and was hospitalized for seven days. He still wheezes on occasion and has a nebulizer that he uses at home as needed. Alex has not been bothered by chronic ear infections or persistent digestive complaints. Alex's pediatrician recently determined that he had excess wax build-up in one ear, but no corrective measures were taken or recommended. Vision raises no concern. He is currently in good health.

Background/Behavioral Observation: Mrs. A described her son as "very bright, but extremely physical." She commented that he seems to crave strong physical movement. He touches everything, loves to be messy, and "puts everything in his mouth." He likes to pound on things with his fists, stomp heavily with his feet, and throw things against the walls. Alex also is very noisy. He likes to let out high-pitched shrieks, and will shriek more loudly when told not to. He loves climbing, running around, and leaping from high places. In general his actions are "risky and scary" according to his mother, and he has to be closely trailed at the playground. However, he is also extremely competent physically and quite sure of his actions. Mrs. A mentioned that he will put an entire popsicle in his mouth and never complain about the cold. He loves rough-housing and tackling others. He also tends to give "tight, strangle-hold kind of hugs."

Alex has been placed in several day care situations, but has been asked to withdraw from each program after just a few weeks, because "he could not manage his behaviors" (the first such incident occurred when he was 22 months old). He was consistently biting other children, grabbing and pulling on their hair, and generally engaging in "safety-compromising behaviors." He now stays under the care of his full-time nanny while his parents are at work. Alex reportedly showed little remorse or empathy when he would behave in this manner. He no longer bites or pulls hair, but essentially shows little interest in playing with peers other than engaging in chasing games.

In terms of self-care, Alex is uncooperative with the dressing process. He can offer some assistance at times, but cannot dress or undress without assistance. He can use utensils to feed himself but strongly prefers to feed himself with his fingers. He likes to eat, but needs to be carefully supervised as he tends to overstuff food in his mouth and there have been several choking incidents as a result. He is toilet trained for the daytime. Alex finds it very difficult to settle down at bedtime, but then sleeps through the night.

I met Alex and Mrs. A in the reception area of the agency's office suite and escorted them back to the evaluation room. Alex was quite animated and smiling and did not appear apprehensive upon meeting me. He made inconsistent eye contact. Alex's body was in constant motion as we worked through the various table-top activities for the fine motor testing. He could not remain seated for more than a minute before he would pop out of his chair. He was talkative, and he clearly used and understood language appropriately. He was essentially cooperative with and interested in the activities, and there were no behavioral or emotional over-reactions of any kind during our visit.

The **Peabody Developmental Motor Scales-2** is used to assess gross and fine motor skills in children from birth to six years old. The fine motor portion assesses grasp, hand-use, eye–hand coordination, and manual dexterity (the manipulation of small objects by use of the hands).

Fine Motor: Alex was able to pick up slender wooden toy candles and insert them into corresponding holes in a toy birthday cake. He was able to pick up pennies one at a time off the table surface and insert each one into a coin slot, even when the orientation of the slot was shifted. However, finger movements were quite stiff during each of these one-handed targeting tasks, and he had a noticeable difficulty relaxing the tension on his fingers as he released each item into its designated target location. Alex was able to stack one-inch blocks ten-high, and made corrections to the alignment as he proceeded. He was able to thread a lace through different-sized buttons and beads and retrieve the string from the other side, a task that requires both hands to perform a different part of the same overall task. He removed the top from a screw-type jar. Alex was able to replicate the simple three-dimensional block structures of a four-block train or a three-block bridge from visual demonstration. Alex held onto a crayon in his right hand with a light thumbs-down fisted grip. He was able to copy a concise line in both a vertical or horizontal orientation, but only a circular scribble. He held scissors correctly and was able to snip into the edge of a piece of paper.

Alex received a standard score of 8 (low-average performance) on the visual-motor subtest, and a 6 (2 standard deviations below age-expected performance) on the grasping subtest of the Peabody. These scores result in a cumulative fine motor quotient of 82. These scores represent mild to moderately concerning scores. However, Alex's heightened activity level and inability to remain seated for these activities seriously bring into question whether he will be able to appropriately access his skill set as he needs to once he is in a structured school program.

Sensory Integration: When professional evaluators look at how well a child's sensory systems are working, we are essentially looking at two main areas of potential difficulties, both of which can dramatically affect how a child behaves and matures developmentally. At one extreme is the child who requires an inordinate amount of some kind of sensory input before a sensory experience "registers" with them and allows them to react with an appropriate response. The other extreme describes children who are acutely sensitive to specific types of sensory experiences. Seemingly normal levels of sound, light, smell, oral experience, or touch may register with them as distracting, uncomfortable, or even distressing.

Based on his parents' responses on the Sensory Profile questionnaire, Alex received significantly elevated scores (in the Definite Difference range) for a Sensory Seeking behavior profile (what is referred to as a High Threshold behavior set). A High Threshold profile refers to a child who needs considerably more emphatic sensory input of one kind or another in order to satisfy a high—and therefore difficult-to-achieve—neurochemical threshold in the brain (a "threshold" refers to the point at which a reaction in the brain generates a response to a stimulus on the part of a child). It is only after such a high threshold is met that the sensory event convincingly "registers," and allows the child to fully appreciate the input and settle into a more comfortable, organized state and a more reasonable activity pace. Such children are aware of this unsatisfying response to stimuli and are generally intent on compensating for this inefficiency. They are very active and constantly scanning their immediate environment for opportunities to more vigorously activate pressure and weight-bearing (proprioceptive) sensory receptors in key weight-bearing joints (thus earning them the description of being "Sensory Seekers," as well as quite distractible).

Mrs. A's responses point out the following persistent behaviors: Alex frequently seeks all kinds of movement and becomes overly excitable during movement activities. He avoids quiet play choices. He touches objects and people excessively, often to the point of irritability. Alex also mouths objects frequently. He deliberately makes loud noises, and finds some way of using his body to heighten his physical contact with his environment (usually involving pushing against things or people, squeezing or hugging them, or pulling against objects). He also shows an unusual need to touch or grab objects, toys, and surfaces. Even his seemingly more aggressive behaviors—including pushing into children and hugging them forcibly—can be interpreted as his need for physical experiences that involve applying pressure and making a strong impact, although he is unfortunately unaware of how inappropriate these actions are. These actions are all impressively consistent with those other behaviors described in the Background section of this report—pounding, stomping, flinging things, extremely tight hugs, tackling and rough-housing all hold the promise of delivering significant input to weight-bearing joints through pressure and resistance. Keep in mind that these responses are all prompted by his poor registration of sensory input. This is further borne out by his insensitivity to having a whole popsicle in his mouth and his scant response to painful events. His slow response to auditory cues also suggests that meeting response thresholds may be extremely difficult for him to achieve at times. These are classic presentations of the Sensory Seeking child. Obviously, this skewed set of priorities can significantly interfere with learning and socialization, and may render his skill set inaccessible when he needs to access it in the school routine.

Summary/Recommendations: Alex is a bright and active young boy being raised in a caring and supportive household. Scores on standardized fine motor testing reflect no serious concerns from a developmental point of view. Of significantly more pressing concern, he convincingly presents with difficulties with impulsivity, Sensory Seeking behaviors, and behaviors that are at times seen as aggressive and that pose potentially serious challenges to his ability to perform his role as a student in a busy classroom. I am therefore strongly recommending that Alex receive occupational therapy at the Committee on Preschool Special Education (CPSE) level to address sensory registration and self-regulation issues. Such services would be most appropriate in a sensory gym that makes suspended equipment and movement opportunities available to him as he works with his therapist. Services should also provide an opportunity to implement a sensory diet designed by his therapist to provide him with regularly scheduled opportunities of additional, appropriate input throughout his day.

THE LOW THRESHOLD/HIGHLY RESPONSIVE CHILD

Almost everyone has at least one outstanding memory of having a really bad case of the flu. When the subject comes up in conversation, you can see this other person almost immediately transported back to that episode. It's as though they have little choice but to re-experience the worst aspects of it. Indulge me for a moment and revisit your own memory of such a time. Put aside the stomach distress, and the awful digestive discharges from one direction or another. Concentrate on just what your body felt like, when the most ambitious undertaking you could deal with was to wait for each long minute to pass until you fell asleep and made it to the next day. Chances are you were in your bed or on the couch, perhaps cold one minute and hot the next. Even the weight and feel of a nice clean cotton sheet was irritating as it dragged along your toes and toenails. Most of the lights in the room had to be dimmed or turned off completely because they otherwise seemed to light up your space like a blast furnace. Even your favorite mellow music played ever so softly felt like a marching band inside your head. You wanted more than anything to watch television, just so the time would pass, but the fleeting, changing images and soundtrack were enough to make you dizzy. And talk about dizzy, your effort to get up and go to the bathroom had to be oh so slow and carefully orchestrated. Otherwise the simple act of changing your head position sent you into a tailspin. And the smells! Everything smelled ghastly. Not just the odors that were the by-products of the flu, but everything—your wife's perfume, the everyday lotions and soaps in the bathroom, the faint smell of fabric softener on the towels and washcloths that you never ever notice on a good day, and even the smell of peanut butter or toast being served up several rooms away. And speaking of food, the simple act of looking at food, let alone smelling or tasting it was enough to make you—well you know the rest.

In a nutshell, your body was screaming to somehow have this onslaught on your senses stop. Even a fraction of such discomfort is something you wouldn't wish on anyone. Fortunately this degree of discomfort happens to most of us only once in a blue moon. But can you imagine what it would be like if even one of your senses felt this assaulted a good deal of the time? This kind of hypersensitivity, to some greater or lesser degree, describes the day-to-day world of some Low Threshold children. Let me take pains to be clear about this analogy. I am not suggesting that such a young one is constantly plagued with flu-like symptoms. What I am describing is the child who is forced to respond to or defend themselves against stimuli that most of us would label harmless and unthreatening on a daily basis.

If you remember, with a Low Threshold condition responses to specific, sensory stimulation are triggered more quickly and dramatically—and therefore frequently— because response thresholds in the brain are met so easily. It's as though the child's mechanism for responding to a sensory event is on a hair trigger. As such, not only are these thresholds reached easily and frequently, but the insistence of processing these events may make even some seemingly benign stimuli overwhelming.

THE SENSORY SENSITIVE CHILD

Similar to our discussion about the High Threshold child, the Low Threshold child's brain may respond to the world around them either passively or actively. The passive response to registering the stimuli describes the Sensory Sensitive child. This child finds it difficult to offer any resistance to the barrage of triggering stimuli. The primary characteristic of this child is that they are unable to effectively habituate (tune out) redundant and unimportant information that is always present. The vast majority of us are able to "triage" or prioritize incoming stimuli based on how routine or important they appear to be. Imagine what it must be like to be compelled to attend to every sound that enters your space as though hearing it for the first time—the fire sirens outside your window, the phone ringing in the next-door apartment, muted voices in the open doorway leading to the classroom. What if you had little choice but to redirect your visual attention to every slight movement or passerby that crossed in front of the glass door of your classroom? And what about that coffee cup with the chipped rim that demands that you be surprised every time you lift it to your mouth? Here's the bottom line: If you had to attend to every detail in your immediate environment—trivial and significant—then the act of maintaining your focus would be next to impossible. Often mistaken for a child with attention deficit, this child is actually the diametric opposite. Instead of not being able to focus on anything, the Sensory Sensitive child is compelled to attend to every trivial trigger event in their world. Admittedly the effect is the same, but the word that more accurately describes this child is "distractible." I myself struggle with this kind of undefended sensitivity. I cannot work on my writing or read a book if there is music playing in the background. It's just impossible to keep it in the background.

The Sensory Sensitive child's head is on a swivel. Obviously, this gets in the way of learning opportunities, focused skill rehearsals that we unconsciously depend on to refine our skill levels, and the sense of being settled that organization and sustained attention bestows upon a child.

TYRONE

(A Sensory Sensitive child)

OCCUPATIONAL THERAPY EVALUATION

Name: Tyrone

Chronological Age: 5 yrs. (60 mos.)

Reason for Referral: Tyrone is being evaluated at the Committee on Preschool Special Education (CPSE) level to assess sensory-motor function and assist in future planning. Tyrone's preschool teacher requested this evaluation due to apparent attention and information processing difficulties.

This occupational therapy evaluation will formally evaluate fine motor and visual-motor abilities (grasp, manipulation of small objects, use of both hands, motor planning and execution, body awareness, eye–hand coordination) as they impact on pre-academic learning readiness and self-care routines; as well as consider whether there are sensory registration or processing difficulties that could result in considerable discomfort, or behaviors that interfere with typical developmental gains or school preparedness.

Site of Evaluation: This afternoon evaluation was conducted at the Head Start facility where Tyrone attends the preschool program. Direct fine motor testing was administered in an unoccupied school room provided by the school. The space was quite adequate in terms of cleanliness, spaciousness, and relative lack of distraction. I spoke with Tyrone's mother by phone several days after my school visit.

Birth/Medical History: Tyrone is the only child of Ms. T (he has very little contact with his father). Ms. T reported that her pregnancy was unremarkable following a good course of pre-natal care. Tyrone was born at full term and came home with his mother. He reportedly cried a lot as an infant. Tyrone was hospitalized for five days in November of 2013 for an asthma attack. He continues to have flare-ups of this condition, mostly during very cold weather. He takes a daily asthma medication and has a nebulizer at home that is used on an as-needed basis. There have been no subsequent hospitalizations, and no significant illnesses or injuries. There is no history of chronic ear infection, persistent digestive complaints, ongoing respiratory issues, or allergies. Hearing and vision raise no significant concerns. He is currently in good health.

Background/Behavioral Observation: Ms. T stated that Tyrone likes to solve problems on his own. He is "determined and excited to learn more." She stated that he is very interested in other children and is quite social. Tyrone has very few opportunities to play with other children of his age outside of school. He enjoys going to the playground, is comfortable using the play apparatus, and has a good sense of safety limits. Tyrone's response to painful incidents is typical.

Ms. T expressed the following concerns about her son. He is distracted very easily and cannot seem to remember basic learning concepts even after rehearsing these numerous times. He cannot say the letters of the alphabet in order and often reverses the letters in his name while writing. In general, she commented that "listening and comprehension" are two significant challenges for Tyrone.

Tyrone's teacher also identified "processing and distractibility" as two of her primary concerns. He reportedly can't sit still on the carpet during group meeting time, and gives verbal answers to questions that are frequently off topic. He cannot complete basic repetitive patterns as would be expected of a child his age. Retention of even basic preschool information is extremely difficult for him, and he requires frequent teacher support to remain on task. He does not have school readiness skills such as knowing his numbers and letters. She claimed that he has recently developed defiance behaviors. Tyrone will also frequently confront other children when they are not following the classroom routine. His teacher added that he still cannot correctly identify major body parts and features. He is reluctant to play some physical games, and his balance and coordination skills seem diminished.

Upon my arrival Tyrone was sitting at a table playing bingo with his class. He did not appear to need a movement break and did not look as though the process was difficult or stressful for him. He continued to sit with several classmates as they listened to a presentation about healthy eating habits, and then followed instructions to make trail mix as a healthy snack. He sat with a calm body, occasionally speaking to one of his neighbors in a soft voice. There were no behavioral or emotional over-reactions to anything during the time I observed him.

Tyrone came willingly with me to the room designated for my testing. He was very friendly and made good eye contact with me. He spoke in clear, complete sentences and appeared to understand everything I said to him. Tyrone was interested in the toys and games that I presented him with for our fine motor testing. He sat calmly for the 25 minutes of testing without the need for a major movement break. Occasionally he was distracted by sounds coming from the hallway, but was easily redirected back to task. He showed a nice emotional range.

The **Peabody Developmental Motor Scales-2** is used to assess gross and fine motor skills in children from birth to six years old. The fine motor portion assesses grasp, hand-use, eye–hand coordination, and manual dexterity (the manipulation of small objects by use of the hands).

Fine Motor: Tyrone was able to pick up slender wooden toy candles and insert them into corresponding holes in a toy birthday cake. He was able to unscrew and replace the top of a small screw-type jar. Tyrone was able to stack blocks ten-high using good visual direction of his hand efforts to make corrections to the alignment of the tower. He was able to copy the simple three-dimensional block designs of a four-block train, a three-block bridge, and a set of steps. He was able to pass a lace through the opening on a large plastic button, turn the button over, and pull the lace through from the other side. Tyrone held a crayon in his left hand with an appropriate pinch grip. He was able to copy a concise vertical line and a horizontal line, a circle, an intersecting cross, and a square (and then was able to color within the perimeter of the square nicely). He traced over a vertical ten-inch line without deviating from the line. He also wrote his first name, but did not use the correct letters to do so. Tyrone held scissors with an appropriate thumbs-up grip. He was able to cut through paper neatly along a straight line, but had more difficulty as he attempted to cut out the perimeter of a two-inch diameter circle. He was able to independently unbutton the buttons on his sweater.

Tyrone received a standard score of 9 (average performance) on both the visual-motor subtest and the grasping subtest of the Peabody. This indicates that there are no remarkable sensory-motor or developmental impairments that interfere with his fine motor skill set.

Sensory Integration: When professional evaluators look at how well a child's sensory systems are working, we are essentially looking at two main areas of potential difficulties, both of which can dramatically affect how a child behaves and matures developmentally. At one extreme is the child who requires an inordinate amount of some kind of sensory input before a sensory experience "registers" with them and allows them to react with an appropriate response. The other extreme describes children who are acutely sensitive to specific types of sensory experiences. Seemingly normal levels of sound, light, smell, or touch may register with them as distracting, uncomfortable, or even distressing.

Based on his teacher's responses on the Sensory Profile questionnaire, Tyrone's scores were in the significant (Definite Difference) range for several of the sensory-influenced behavior profiles and sensory processing sections considered. Most notably, scores were significantly elevated for both a sensory-influenced Low Registration pattern of behaviors, as well as for a Sensory Sensitivity profile of behaviors.

The Low Registration (or Poor Registration) child exhibits difficulties in efficiently registering certain types of sensory input. That is to say, they cannot fully meet specific high—difficult-to-achieve—chemical thresholds in the brain that relay information about a specific sensory event, and the sensory experience therefore does not convincingly "register" (a "threshold" in this context refers to that point at which enough sensory input has been processed in the brain to generate a response to the stimulus). Such a child typically needs considerably more sensory input of one kind or another before they can satisfy their difficult-to-achieve neurological thresholds, and only then fully appreciate, or "register," the input of that bodily experience.

These children appear physically unsettled, and generally are very active. These behaviors are consistent with school reports that Tyrone frequently can't sit still and fidgets a great deal during group activities. His teacher reports that he seeks out all kinds of physical and movement opportunities and activities to the point that it interferes with his daily routines, and he is frequently "on the go." He also has a frequent practice of touching other people to the point where it irritates them. He fiddles with objects in his hands a lot. These types of activities point out his difficulties in efficiently registering strong input from his environment. In a similar vein, poor registration of auditory input may help to explain why Tyrone routinely misses auditory cues and seems to ignore directions and cues from the staff as reported by his teacher (to the point of seeming "oblivious" at times). Even though auditory acuity appears intact, he may simply not be meeting the thresholds for these auditory events to sufficiently register, and therefore is not prepared with an appropriate and timely response to cues.

With the above assessment noted, it is important to point out that, as I observed him in the classroom and in our direct one-to-one interaction during testing, Tyrone remained calmly seated for the duration of these 30-minute activities. He did not require frequent shifts in position or movement breaks of any kind, and he carried on regulated, soft-spoken, and appropriate conversations with his peers. What I did observe was how easily distracted Tyrone was by even the slightest sound from the perimeter of (or just outside of) the room during activities. This speaks more to the point of his elevated scores for Sensory Sensitivity. The Sensitive child does not have the ability to filter out redundant or unimportant information from his immediate environment. They appear as though they are unable to prioritize what sensory information is important to them and what is not. As such, they are essentially forced to respond to even the slightest, unrelated stimulus, appearing extremely distractible in the process, and perhaps significantly interfering with their short-term memory. The teacher's responses on the Sensory Profile questionnaire attest to this. Tyrone is easily distracted in the classroom throughout his day. He startles rather easily when others come unexpectedly in contact with him. Tyrone also appears to notice everything that is going on around him by vigilantly scanning the room for activities that might be important, even small changes in the physical space, and by policing the actions of his classmates. The Sensitive child is not only forced to attend to these changes, but is also discomforted by them since they are most at ease when things are routine, predictable, and unchanging. The child faced with so many interruptions during skill rehearsal is clearly at a disadvantage in terms of motor or developmental skill acquisition. Overall, these behaviors have the potential to seriously interfere with learning readiness and skill acquisition, appropriate socialization, and his ability to participate in important structured routines at school.

Summary/Recommendations: Tyrone is a healthy, friendly, and active young boy being raised in a caring and supportive household. His standardized scores on the Peabody for fine motor ability represent a solid age-appropriate skill set of fine motor abilities (despite his apparent struggle with basic learning concepts such as writing the correct letters to his name—this is not a fine motor difficulty). Teacher reports and scores on standardized sensory testing point out difficulties with being able to efficiently process and register certain types of sensory input, as well as heightened sensitivity to seemingly random sensory influences. This results in heightened activity levels in the classroom and high distractibility that seems to impact on his learning preparedness.

I am therefore recommending that Tyrone receive occupational therapy to address his sensory registration and self-regulation difficulties. Hopefully this will address sensory issues that may interfere with his work, activity, and activity levels while in school. Tyrone would also benefit from the services of a Special Education Itinerant Teacher (a one-to-one educator) qualified to offer him support and redirect him when necessary while in school.

THE SENSORY AVERSE CHILD

After performing literally hundreds of occupational therapy evaluations with young children it is my opinion that the Sensory Averse child is the poster child for the community of children with Sensory Processing Disorders. Frequently, when I've introduced the topic of Sensory Integration with a parent, these are the children that they have heard about and seem to understand somewhat. Not surprisingly, the discussion is often reduced to "those kids who can't stand having tags in their shirts." Think back on our little flu exercise of just a few pages ago. The Sensory Averse child's experience of even something as simple as walking barefoot in sand, brushing their teeth, or tolerating clothing tags may be so exaggerated as to be distinctly uncomfortable, threatening, or even painful.

The Sensory Averse child offers perhaps the most active resistance to their sensory registration process. As the label implies, this child's behaviors clearly reflect their efforts to ward off potentially bothersome stimuli of one kind or another. This young one is quite vigilant in most situations, often stubborn or willful, withdrawn from most social situations, and comfortable primarily in only the most familiar and predictable settings. To look at them you realize that this child's facial expression and body language is frequently "on guard." They may have a stern facial countenance and may choose to retreat to overseeing a small, sedentary personal space that can be more easily controlled. These are the kids who remain on the periphery of the group, and may slightly recoil as someone advances towards them. They may insist on being first or last in line so they are not as likely to come into body contact with their neighbor.

They can also be very stubborn. They want to be in control as much as possible to make events as predictable as possible. Here's the rule: No surprises, no curve balls. Any change in their routine is recognized as an invitation for possibly noxious or bothersome trigger events to enter their space. Teachers often make the comment that transitions are difficult. Sensory Averse children are certainly not the most social kids in the classroom and tend to be extremely apprehensive with strangers. And similar to your attitude when you had the flu, they can be downright cranky a lot of the time, and find it difficult to regain their composure, especially since they repeat this exercise so frequently.

I find that more than any of the other sensory behavior patterns that we have looked at, the Sensory Averse child may be struggling primarily with one of his sensory pathways. That means that their poor tolerance levels for processing information is much more specific to processing auditory signals, or visual signals, or just tactile signals, and so on. It is much more of a signature. The children I've evaluated appear to be much easier for a parent or teacher to get a handle on. Little Joey's problem is that he can't tolerate noise of any kind. Miranda's the kind of little girl who won't even let her parents or grandparents touch her without protest. Max can't stand to have his feet off the ground in any number of different situations. It's entirely possible, of course, for the hypersensitive child to have a dramatic reaction to several different types of stimulation, but usually there is a primary area of concern.

Here then are some of the behavioral consequences confronting the Sensory Averse child that are associated with each of the primary sensory pathways.

Auditory

It's not just loud noises that bother the defensive child. Most of us don't enjoy that experience very much. Instead, even seemingly routine elevations of sound levels can make this child cringe and try to protect themselves. Traffic noises, motoric noises, and vacuum cleaners, not to mention the everyday din of the busy classroom, can stop this child in their tracks, frequently causing them to cover their ears, and perhaps even try to drown out the noise with odd noises that they make themselves. Parents report that this makes it especially difficult to bring their child to age-appropriate concert events, children's theater, or amusement parks, not to mention birthday parties with their celebratory auditory pitch. As soon as these children are old enough to realize what these invitations mean, they are likely to resist going with everything they can muster.

Visual

These children find even seemingly benign levels of light bothersome. They may cover their eyes or squint in normal daylight, usually accompanied by some complaint. It's not unusual for these children to prefer to be in the dark. It's interesting to note that some parents with a visually defensive child will somewhat unknowingly learn to accommodate their child. Lighting levels in their home are generally muted, and even paint selections tend to be neutral rather than bold and vibrant.

Atypical responses to visual sensitivity are not strictly related to light intensity either. Moving and changing images paraded in front of a child at close range can often bring on a dramatic response on the part of the Sensory Sensitive or Defensive child. Consider how powerful the effects of television images are. I am no longer surprised when a mom tells me that her hyperactive, poorly focused son or daughter can sit in front of the TV or a video game for hours at a time, as though that was proof that attention and self-regulation are really not their issues. The truth is that moving visual images are tremendously powerful influences on the brain, especially that of a truly defensive child. In some cases this challenges the child's ability to regulate their response to the stimulus, resulting in unregulated movement levels of their own.

Oral

These are the children who either display little interest in food or quite clearly demonstrate that they don't like to eat most foods. They are the extremely picky eater, generally satisfying themselves with small amounts of food, and usually limiting themselves to the same few foods that they can tolerate. They won't even try new foods. Meal times may go on for hours, and the child needs to be distracted before each bite of food is swallowed. Self-help skills such as using utensils to feed themselves may be delayed, because the child simply has little interest in developing the skill. Such children often do not tolerate tooth brushing, and making a visit to the dentist can be truly a nightmare.

There is an interesting corollary between the orally defensive child and one who has a significant history of digestive problems. More often than not in my experience, the parent who describes such poor eating habits also reports during our interview that their child had a significant history of Gastric Reflux as an infant. The interesting part is that it begs the entire question of what causes some of these children to be so hyper-responsive to parts of their world. The available literature speculates that while some of these predispositions are genetically determined, they can also be brought on by prematurity, birth trauma, or a significant, protracted health episode. In my mind, the thought of a young child who consistently throws up after every feeding for nine months or so certainly meets the criteria of a protracted medical challenge. This child is the perfect candidate to become an orally defensive child even several years after medication seems to have controlled the reflux condition. Some associations linger forever and help shape who we are.

Vestibular

Remember, vestibular messages are strong signals sent to the brain every time our head moves decidedly out of the vertical, causing normal fluid levels in the inner ear to brush against receptors that line the walls of that structure. For the Low Threshold child, these messages can be overwhelming. Their response is to anticipate, avoid, and/or protest any movement activities that involve having their head displaced from that erect position. The likely offenses would include being laid on their back for a diaper change, and having their head tipped back to wash their hair. These kids are also not the ideal candidates for gymnastics class since somersaults would decidedly trip this mechanism.

Many swinging activities may also trigger this powerful mechanism for the defensive child (try to swing a half-full glass of water in front of you without having the water level splash along the sides). As such, many of these children are fearful of swings on playgrounds, merry-go-rounds, and even some sliding activities. Some even reach the point where any activity that insists on having their feet off the ground, or on an unstable or changing elevation (like a swinging bridge at the playground or climbing stairs), deprives them of that fixed, level, grounded sense of security, and causes them great discomfort and even panic. Needless to say, car rides and boat rides may have the same effect.

Tactile

Can you imagine a small child who is so uncomfortable being touched that they cannot tolerate most forms of physical comfort and affection from even their parents? No hugs, no cuddles (I immediately feel bad for the poor grandparents). These children in general recoil from physical contact that they do not initiate, and particularly from light or unexpected touch. They may rage out at the slightest provocation of this kind, in some cases running the risk of seeming to be emotionally unstable. They are very particular about clothing. They frequently insist on keeping their favorite clothes or soft pajamas on (but get those footed pajamas out of here!).

Back to where our discussion started, they are bothered by some clothing features (tags, elastic) or certain fabrics or textures. The Sensory Averse child is opposed to walking barefoot on most surfaces, and may have a very important set of slippers that need to go everywhere with them. They may be particularly sensitive to water temperature. Daily grooming and wash routines can be especially challenging, especially those that occur throughout the day such as washing their hands and face. Having their nails cut, hair washed, and teeth brushed, getting a haircut, as well as are also potentially traumatic scenarios. The dressing process can predictably lead to a wrestling match and end with the parent doing all the work amidst their child's protests.

Some children seem to have a particularly acute aversion to having pressure applied to their hands. These children will work their hardest not to hold an adult's hand when walking on the street or descending stairs. They may also hold a pencil or crayon with an extremely wispy grip, making it possible for them to leave only the faintest drawing impressions on paper, and greatly compromising their control of the instrument.

In a school setting, the Sensory Averse child is the one who refuses to handle art materials (finger paints, glue, playdough), and won't play in the sensory table (a bin filled with rice, sand, beans, or even shaving cream). It is not unusual for this child to freak out if clothing gets even slightly wet or dirty.

A typical school day with a Sensory Averse child can present a caretaker with many forest fires to put out. And once again, the look on their faces can easily convince you that they're neither comfortable nor enjoying themselves in such a dynamic setting. How challenging it is to think about how ill at ease such a child can be at the very beginning of their school career. In every case these sensitivities have to be respected and treated with care.

SCOTT, PEYTON, AND NEAL

(Sensory Averse children)

OCCUPATIONAL THERAPY EVALUATION

Name: Scott

Chronological Age: 2 yrs., 9 mos. (33 mos.)

Reason for Referral: Scott is receiving this occupational therapy evaluation to assess sensory-motor functioning and assist in future planning. Initial concerns focused on late speech development and delayed onset of motor milestones. Private speech therapies were procured at about 13 months of age and continued for the next 5 months. More recently, concerns voiced by Scott's preschool cite that he often freezes during social contact, doesn't respond when spoken to, isn't actively participating in the group routines and activities, and isn't interacting with peers. Scott was privately reassessed by his prior speech therapist who suggested a consultation with a developmental pediatrician. The pediatrician in turn recommended occupational therapy for sensory processing issues and core weakness.

An occupational therapy evaluation will formally evaluate fine motor and visual-motor skills as well as consider whether there are sensory registration, processing, or self-regulation difficulties that could result in atypical behaviors that interfere with developmental gains.

Site of Evaluation: This afternoon evaluation was conducted in one of the evaluation rooms in the evaluation agency office suite. The space was quite suitable for the evaluations given in terms of spaciousness, cleanliness, and lack of distraction. Ms. S remained with her son throughout the evaluation activities.

Birth/Medical History: Scott is the only child of Mr. and Ms. S. Ms. S reported that her full-term pregnancy was unremarkable. Scott was delivered via an uncomplicated delivery and did not require any additional hospitalization. Ms. S recounted how Scott suffered from Gastric Reflux from about one month of age until about six months of age and was administered medicine. He was identified with low oral muscle tone and drooled a lot. He has not been bothered by ongoing respiratory complaints or chronic ear infections. There have been no subsequent hospital visits, serious injuries, or illnesses. Hearing was tested at one year and found to be within normal ranges. Vision raises no remarkable concerns.

Background/Behavioral Observation: Ms. S described her son as "very smart and quite verbal at home." He enjoys having books read to him and doing rather complicated puzzles (he can work on one for 30 minutes or more). However, Scott can be quite inflexible and rigid about having things done the same way and in the same order, and gets locked into things. He has a particularly heightened focus on numbers and is "obsessed" with elevator control panels. He does not accept physical affection from anyone who is not a family member. Scott is consistently distressed by most grooming routines and refuses to play with play materials such as playdough or shaving cream (Scott will typically "shut down" when exposed to any such new materials). He cannot tolerate being in crowded or noisy environments. Scott takes a while to warm up to other children in small, playdate sessions at home, but then engages with familiar friends.

Scott has been attending preschool classes two afternoons a week for three-hour sessions. His school has issued strong concerns about his level of withdrawal from peer interaction and group activities. He freezes when spoken to and often doesn't seem able to respond to verbal prompts and questions. He doesn't actively participate in the group activities, and will shut down when approached by peers. He seems to find comfort in activities that involve numbers, but may also become hyper-focused on clock numbers and the elevator. Scott shuts down when the group is brought to a larger space in the school for an activity. Ms. S contrasted such consistent behaviors at school with Scott's accounts of his school days. He will talk about the events of his school day "a mile a minute" when he gets home, and seems to want to communicate that he enjoys his time there. His teachers have strongly recommended that Scott be accompanied to school by a Special Education Itinerant Teacher (a one-to-one educator).

I met Scott and his mother in the reception area of the agency office suite. He appeared clearly apprehensive in this novel environment and stayed quite close to his mother. He was convinced to sit in the child chair opposite me in the evaluation room for the test activities. At one point I stood up and moved slightly behind him, and as my arm accidentally touched his he startled and flinched conspicuously. Scott looked directly at me with his eyes wide open and a serious expression on his face almost the whole time, although there were moments when he was able to relax and enjoy the activities presented to him. Most of these instances occurred when I was able to introduce a number into the activity (a countdown for a rocket ship, or a certain number printed on a toy that I brought to his attention). In these cases he would relax and smile and engage more enthusiastically with the activity. He was verbal, but didn't speak much, and he clearly understood what was being said to him. There were no significant behavioral or emotional over-reactions during our visit.

The **Peabody Developmental Motor Scales-2** is used to assess gross and fine motor skills in children from birth to six years old. The fine motor portion assesses grasp, hand-use, eye–hand coordination, and manual dexterity (the manipulation of small objects by use of the hands).

Fine Motor: Scott was able to pick up slender wooden toy candles and insert them into corresponding holes in a toy cake. He was able to pick up pennies one at a time and place them through a coin slot, even when the orientation of the slot was shifted to challenge his wrist rotation and visual direction of his efforts. For both of these one-handed targeting tasks Scott used the fingers on the pinky side of his hand opposed by his thumb rather than an index-finger pincer grip. (Developmentally the pinky side of the hand offers strength and control before the refined use of the index finger-pincer grip develops. Children with core weakness will still rely on this sense of enhanced strength offered by using the outer fingers for a greater sense of stability that their core does not offer them.) Scott unscrewed and replaced the top of a small screw-type jar. He was able to tower one-inch blocks ten-high, but the alignment of the tower was precarious. As he stacked each block he conspicuously held his unused hand out with his fingers splayed and tensed (this is another strategy to enhance the child's sense of control over their hand movements by deliberately summoning tension into the extremity). He was able to replicate the three-dimensional block designs of a four-block train and a three-block bridge with the assistance of minimal verbal cues. Scott held a crayon with his extended fingers pursed around the crayon shaft like the chuck of a drill. In this manner he essentially dragged the crayon across the page. He was able to replicate straight, concise lines, but not in the (horizontal or vertical) orientation that I drew for him. He did not consistently anchor the paper with his non-drawing hand, causing the page to shift and buckle on occasion. Scott did not know how to hold or use scissors.

Scott's performance, based on the Peabody, resulted in a standard score of 7 (between 1 and 2 standard deviations below age-expected performance) on both the visual-motor subtest and the grasping subtest. This results in an overall fine motor quotient of 82 (the typical range is between 90 and 100), indicating mild to moderate concerns with fine motor ability. However, the quality and efficiency of his hand and finger movements appear impacted by his diminished torso stability, leading him to adapt with a variety of tensed, whole hand, and fisted grips that limit and lock his finger movements.

Sensory Integration: When professional evaluators look at how well a child's sensory systems are working, we are essentially looking at two main areas of potential difficulties, both of which can dramatically affect how a child behaves and matures developmentally. At one extreme is the child who requires an inordinate amount of some kind of sensory input before a sensory experience "registers" with them and allows them to react with an appropriate response. The other extreme describes children who are acutely sensitive to specific types of sensory experiences. Seemingly normal levels of sound, light, smell, oral experience, or touch may register with them as distracting, uncomfortable, or even distressing.

The **Infant Toddler Sensory Profile** is a parent response-based questionnaire that provides a method for professionals to measure how efficiently a child registers important sensory information through each of their senses—auditory, visual, tactile, vestibular, proprioceptive (through pressure on muscles and joints), and oral. It also considers clusters of behaviors that are consistent with children who exhibit especially heightened or diminished responses to these sensory trigger events.

According to the results of the caretaker-based Sensory Profile questionnaire, Scott achieved a significantly heightened score for both a Sensory Avoidance and Sensory Sensitivity behavior profile. Both profiles reflect a Low Neurological Threshold condition in which responses to specific, seemingly benign sensory stimulation are triggered more quickly and dramatically—and therefore frequently—because thresholds are met so easily (a "threshold" in this context refers to that point at which enough sensory input has been processed in the brain to generate a response to the stimulus, with the Low Threshold child requiring very little stimulus of one kind or another before the child is forced to respond). This is consistent with Ms. S's reports about her son, both currently and dating back to the time he was an infant. She commented that he is consistently agitated during grooming routines, including having his hair washed and his head tipped back during shampooing. He gets extremely upset when his face and nose need to be wiped. Scott doesn't tolerate walking barefoot on different surfaces. He also dislikes brushing his teeth. Scott will not accept physical affection from anyone other than a family member. As mentioned, Scott cannot tolerate playing with typical age-appropriate materials and substances such as shaving cream and playdough. He also demonstrates auditory sensitivities, as he startles (to both sound and unexpected touch) very easily, and tries to escape from noisy environments.

Ms. S also claims that his behavior deteriorates remarkably when his schedule and routine changes and he wants to be in control of many situations. Keep in mind that a child with significant sensitivities will often try earnestly to gain as much control over a situation as possible (as a way of making the situation as predictable as possible). They cannot easily tolerate changes in plans, expectations, or routines, as any such changes may introduce potentially bothersome input that they cannot accommodate to. Transitions, especially unscheduled ones, are therefore quite difficult. It should come as no surprise that the dependable and predictable outcomes of numbers appeal greatly to Scott. These children are certainly capable of enjoying themselves when in a secure setting, but they often appear vigilant and anxious as they guard against potentially bothersome input in social or novel situations, and may withdraw as a way of further protecting that space. This too is consistent with reports that Scott frequently withdraws from a group situation, and usually avoids playing with other children.

Parents frequently look for explanations for their child's exaggerated defensiveness to aspects of their environment.

Clearly, there is no one answer that clarifies such unique and complex individuals. A child's apparent anxiety may be partly in response to a significant medical history that is characterized by ongoing discomfort (such as protracted bouts of Reflux). In such a scenario, these longstanding discomforts can eventually permeate one's entire disposition, and inclines the child to approach all but the most secure and familiar settings with apprehension and reluctance. Similarly, such defensiveness may be the result of some early trauma that can't be put to rest. It is my informed opinion based on my experience that some children are simply born with a highly responsive sensory/nervous system that predisposes them to immediately guard against perceived threats in their immediate environment. Here is what they all share in common: Our normal day-to-day engagements are governed by the frontal area of our brain that we depend on for judgments, reasoning, and limit-setting. When faced with an imminent threat, blood flow is diverted to the more primitive part of our brain that automatically engages our protective fight or flight mechanisms. But if this stress or "alarm system on" becomes chronic, our "reasonable brain" goes into "sleep mode." Under these conditions global brain management is handed over to the emergency systems which really only do a good job during emergencies. What this leaves is a brain that eventually responds too quickly and too strongly to stimuli (even those stimuli that are not very important). Scott seems to fit this category. Obviously, this level of anxiety has the potential to seriously interfere with aspects of his development.

Summary/Recommendations: Scott is a bright, but extremely cautious, little boy being raised in an obviously caring household. Scores on developmental testing for fine motor ability, as well as direct observation of hand use, raise modest to moderate concerns that are further amplified when the quality and efficiency of his hand strategies are considered. This is in large part due to the effects of his diminished core strength and stability. Of greater concern, standardized scores for sensory processing represented strong aversive responses to numerous aspects of his sensory environment, and likely contribute to his inflexibility, strict adherence to familiar routines, and social withdrawal. These all have the potential to seriously interfere with his subsequent learning opportunities. I am therefore recommending occupational therapy services for Scott at the Committee on Preschool Special Education (CPSE) level, preferably in a sensory gym that can support his fine motor development, strengthen his core stability, and help him to better tolerate sensory input. Discussion should also focus on additional, individual adult support that can be provided to him during his longer school week next term.

OCCUPATIONAL THERAPY EVALUATION

Name: Peyton

Chronological Age: 2 yrs., 10 mos. (34 mos.)

Reason for Referral: Peyton is receiving this occupational therapy evaluation as she prepares to age out of Early Intervention services and formally reach preschool age, and to assist with future planning. Concerns focus primarily on the potential impact of her low muscle tone on her ability to participate in the school environment, as well as some stimming behaviors. She currently receives the following related services through the Early Intervention program: physical therapy—2 x 30 minutes/week, occupational therapy—2 x 30 minutes/week, and speech therapy—2 x 30 minutes/week.

This occupational therapy evaluation will formally evaluate fine motor and visual-motor abilities (grasp, manipulation of small objects, use of both hands, motor planning and execution, body awareness, eye–hand coordination) as they impact on pre-academic learning readiness and self-care routines; as well as consider whether there are sensory registration, processing, or self-regulation difficulties responsible for considerable discomfort, or behaviors that interfere with typical developmental gains or school preparedness.

Site of Evaluation: This afternoon evaluation was conducted in one of the evaluation rooms in the agency office suite. The space was quite suitable for the evaluations given in terms of spaciousness, cleanliness, and lack of distraction. Ms. P remained with her daughter throughout the evaluation activities, and remained following the testing for the parent interview.

Birth/Medical History: Peyton is the only child of Mr. and Ms. P. Ms. P reported that she had Placenta Previa during her pregnancy and had to deliver Peyton at 36 weeks due to her high blood pressure. Peyton was a very small baby and feeding "was a challenge" at first. Hearing and vision have been tested and raise no remarkable concern. There have been no subsequent hospitalizations, serious illnesses, or injuries. Peyton was initially evaluated through the Early

Intervention program at 11 months of age for low muscle tone. Occupational therapy services were awarded approximately six months ago to address some hand-stimming behaviors and her poor ability to cope with certain situations. She has not been troubled by recurring ear infections, ongoing respiratory issues, or persistent digestive complaints. She is currently in good health.

Background/Behavioral Observation: Ms. P described Peyton as "very smart and focused, well behaved," and having a good sense of humor. She is quite detail oriented. Peyton has had a best friend since she was four months old and spends a considerable amount of exclusive time with her. In terms of self-care Peyton can feed herself with a fork but prefers to be fed. She has just started to show an interest in toilet training. Her sleep at night can be quite restless.

Ms. P indicated that Peyton is reluctant to engage with most other little children her age. She is resistant to try new things and transitions can be difficult, at times leading to behavioral breakdowns (several times a day), and the stimming behaviors noted (she clenches her fists and hikes her shoulders), that also present when she is excited. Ms. P also described her concerns about Peyton's motor abilities and low muscle tone. She is reluctant to engage with playground equipment and tends to remain on the periphery. She doesn't walk evenly, has an immature running style, appears clumsy, and is prone to tripping and falling. Peyton still needs close supervision on stairs. Ms. P described Peyton as "fearful and cautious" most of the time, and noted that she "doesn't appear comfortable in her body."

I met Ms. P and Peyton in the agency reception area. Peyton appeared quite apprehensive about the situation and stayed very close to her mother. Peyton would not sit in the child's chair opposite me and instead remained on her mother's lap for the first part of our activities. She answered some of my questions with single words that indicated that she understood and used language somewhat purposefully. She needed some coaxing to try the activities with the brightly colored toys that I brought out, but became more relaxed by the time we nearly completed the testing. There were no behavioral over-reactions of any kind during my visit.

Gross Motor/Neuromotor Assessment: Peyton walks with a gangly, somewhat uneven gait. She cannot jump with both feet off the floor at the same time and is especially cautious on stairs (she still needs hand-held supervision).

Muscle tone is low in Peyton's trunk and upper extremities (her muscles feel more flaccid than firm when challenged or when resistance is applied). Hand strength is diminished.

There was no observable evidence of tremor or rapid involuntary eye movement that might signal further neurological involvement.

The **Peabody Developmental Motor Scales-2** is used to assess gross and fine motor skills in children from birth to six years old. The fine motor portion assesses grasp, hand-use, eye–hand coordination, and manual dexterity (the manipulation of small objects by use of the hands).

Fine Motor: Peyton was able to pick up toy birthday candles and insert them into their corresponding holes in a toy cake. She was able to insert a number of coins into the slot on the bank surface, even when I deliberately shifted the orientation of the slot to challenge her wrist position and her visual attention to the task. As she did both of these tasks, she tensed and splayed the fingers of her non-involved hand (a common strategy to which low-tone children resort to summon tension into their extremities to give them a more convincing sense of postural stability during task attempts). She was able to remove and replace the top of a small screw-type jar. Peyton was able to very slowly and deliberately pass a lace through the opening in a large toy button, turn the button over, and pull the lace out through the other side. She stacked one-inch blocks nine-high. As she did so she held each block with her pinky and ring fingers (the pinky side of the hand is relied on more for strength tasks than the index finger side with which we develop our comfortable, precision movements). Peyton held a crayon in her right hand with a pronated, thumbs-down fisted grip. In this manner she was able to copy concise lines in a vertical and horizontal direction and a nearly closed, spherical circle. She held scissors with an appropriate thumbs-up grip and was able to cut into a piece of paper (not just along the edge as would be developmentally expected).

Peyton achieved a standard score of 9 (average) on the visual-motor subtest and a standard score of 8 (low average performance) on the grasping subtest. These scores are typically well within the average range for fine motor performance. It is important to more closely consider the limitations of the test's "developmental" frame of reference. The Peabody awards points when a child is able to accomplish each of the task challenges. However, the test does not look at the kinds of strategies the child employs to accomplish the task, nor does it consider the quality of the task attempt. For example, it does not comment on tensed arm and hand strategies that limit the independent movements of the elbow, wrist, and finger joints. Nor does it subtract points when a child uses compensatory strategies to stabilize their posture, as Peyton consistently did with her choice of grips and non-involved hand clenching. Such actions clearly point out the effects of Peyton's low tone and postural instability. Until she makes improvements in further strengthening her core muscle groups, she will likely continue to approach fine motor tasks with the same limitations, even as these tasks become increasingly more complex and demanding. Certainly, from a developmental point of view Peyton is clever enough to problem solve and accomplish a number of these task challenges (especially more so in a comfortable, familiar setting). But from a strength/weakness outlook, the quality and efficiency of her execution is compromised. In a matter of literally a few more months her current approaches to these kinds of tasks would result in scores that would be more concerning.

Sensory Integration: From a sensory integrative point of view, learning begins when a person receives accurate sensory information from sight, hearing, smell, taste, touch, movement, and pressure through their joints and muscles (proprioception). When specific "sensations" register properly and are efficiently relayed to the brain, the person can then process this information, and use it to organize behaviors and responses. For some children this process is disrupted. As a result they may be either hypersensitive or under-responsive to specific sensory stimuli. A child with heightened sensitivities may experience certain sensory experiences as constantly distracting, uncomfortable, threatening, or even painful. Other children have such a low sensitivity to specific stimuli that they register these impressions very little or not at all, or may be motivated to compensate on their own in order to satisfy these difficult-to-achieve thresholds. In either case, their ability to create appropriate responses is disrupted.

The **Infant Toddler Sensory Profile** provides a standardized method for professionals to measure how well a child registers, processes, and self-regulates sensory information. Its purpose is to evaluate the possible effects of sensory processing on the child's daily performance patterns and to provide information about which sensory systems might be contributing to or creating barriers to functional performance.

Based on her mother's responses on the Sensory Profile questionnaire, Peyton achieved significantly heightened scores (in the Definite Difference range) for a Sensation Avoidance behavior profile. This is referred to as a Low Threshold behavior set. A Low Neurological Threshold condition describes a condition in which responses to seemingly benign sensory stimulation are triggered more quickly and dramatically—and therefore frequently—because thresholds are met so easily (a "threshold" refers to the point at which a neurochemical reaction in the brain forces it to respond to a stimulus). This is consistent with Ms. P's reports that Peyton consistently becomes upset if her face, hands, or clothing get messy and will protest having her face washed or wiped. She protests grooming activities, especially having her head tipped back to wash her hair and having her nails trimmed. She has a difficult time being placed on her back onto a cold or rough surface, and rebels at walking barefoot on certain surfaces. Peyton also startles easily at sound, and is extremely uncomfortable in crowded situations. She also reportedly has considerable difficulty in tolerating changes in her routines, and engaging in new activities. Children with hypersensitivity to their environment depend on a familiar and consistent routine as a way of predicting and preparing for what comes into their personal space. As such, transitions are particularly difficult for these children. The Sensory Avoidant child also typically has an especially difficult time in modulating their emotional responses to sensory events that they find disturbing (modulation refers to a child's ability to react to a sensory stressor with an appropriate and measured emotional response). These children frequently impress others as shy or anxious.

I find it important to address Peyton's apparent apprehension to aspects of her routine and environment from another vantage point. Perhaps her most outstanding focus of concern is her weak core strength, impacting conspicuously on gross motor accomplishment, but also adding another level of stressor to peer interaction. The child with diminished stability in their torso will typically be apprehensive in play situations (especially among active peers), not only because they are aware of their postural vulnerability but also because the act of intentionally summoning enough tension in their trunk muscles to stabilize themselves is a difficult and unpleasant task. Not only is that a daunting task, but such repeated encounters can make the astute child self-conscious of their ability to manage it. The result very well could be a reluctance to engage socially and the emotional frustration that accompanies that self-awareness. It is interesting to note that most of the "sensory" stressors that seem to consistently elicit a negative response from Peyton—washing her face, placing her on her back to change a diaper, tipping her head back to shampoo—all involve her caretaker applying pressure directly on her body, often to deliberately shift her body position. Most children are prepared for these transitional movements because their muscle tone is in a state of readiness at all times. The child with particularly low tone and poor postural stability is particularly vulnerable to such challenges and cannot prepare or steady themselves for even such seemingly benign postural adjustments. It's plausible that the child who is aware of such physical challenges, especially in the dynamic preschool setting or on the playground, will respond fearfully or remain on the periphery of a group of peers. Interestingly, their learned response to such challenges is to brace themselves, by stiffening and by clenching their hands and compressing their neck into their shoulders, very much like the kinds of stimming behaviors described by Ms. P. With this all considered, it is my opinion that except in the most comfortable and familiar settings Peyton quickly adopts a defensive posture at times accompanied by anxious responses to simple physical challenges. This learned behavior then becomes readily available to her when other stressors are encountered (including those that seem to be exclusively sensory in nature). As such, it is difficult to ascertain to what extent Peyton's responses are attributed to sensory triggers, or whether those responses are simply a patent response to challenge in general in which her fight or flight response kicks in quickly.

Summary/Recommendations: Peyton is a retiring, but interested, little girl on the verge of her school career, being raised in an obviously caring household. Average standard scores for Fine Motor ability would seem to indicate no apparent delays in her skill set. Peyton knows how to problem solve her way through most task challenges commendably. However, because of her significant core weakness and instability she has learned to recruit a number of compensatory, inefficient hand strategies that may require retraining as she works on her strength and stability. I am therefore recommending that Peyton continue to receive occupational therapy services at her current mandate in a gym setting. This will also allow for additional observation of her sensory status.

OCCUPATIONAL THERAPY EVALUATION

Name: Neal

Chronological Age: 2 yrs., 9 mos. (33 mos.)

Reason for Referral: Neal is receiving this OT evaluation as he prepares to age out of the Early Intervention program and to assess sensory-motor function to assist with future educational planning. Neal and his twin sister were born prematurely at 31 weeks' gestation. He started to receive services through the Early Intervention program at one year of age. He currently receives the following services through Early Intervention: physical therapy—2 x 30 minutes/week, and occupational therapy—2 x 30 minutes/week (supplemented by once-weekly private sessions in a sensory gym that address reported vestibular processing challenges). He had been receiving speech therapy, but the service was discontinued.

An occupational therapy evaluation will formally evaluate fine motor and visual-motor skills as well as consider whether there are sensory registration, processing, or self-regulation difficulties that could result in atypical behaviors that interfere with developmental gains.

Site of Evaluation: This afternoon evaluation was conducted in one of the evaluation rooms in the agency office suite. The space was quite suitable for the evaluations given in terms of spaciousness, cleanliness, and lack of distraction. Ms. N accompanied her son and remained with him throughout the evaluation visit.

Birth/Medical History: Neal and his twin sister are the only children of Mr. and Ms. N. The twins were born at 31 weeks' gestation and delivered via emergency cesarean procedure. Both children remained in the Neonatal Intensive Care Unit for one month. Neal briefly received oxygen support and light therapy for jaundice. He was also fed through a nasogastric tube for several weeks. It was determined that both twins had suffered a Grade 1 (least severe) Intraventricular Hemorrhage (a minor bleeding event in the brain ventricles). Neal also had Torticollis and Plagiocephaly as an infant (Ms. N speculated that these conditions may have affected the vestibular mechanisms of Neal's inner ear, as he hates the movement of being on a swing, car rides, having his head tipped out of position, or anything that upsets his center of gravity). At three months of age both children developed Gastric Reflux symptoms and were administered Zantac (Neal continued to take it until he was approximately one year old). He has also been bothered with bouts of "pretty bad constipation" according to Ms. N. Neal reportedly has no sense of when his stomach is sated and continues to eat until stopped by an adult (and will then protest). He has not been troubled by ongoing respiratory complaints or chronic ear infections. There are no conspicuous concerns with his hearing. Ms. N stated that she was told that Neal should anticipate glasses as he gets older as his vision tested "borderline." There have been no subsequent hospitalizations, serious illnesses, or injuries for either child. Neal has been diagnosed with very low muscle tone throughout his body (his mother described him as "floppy when picked up"). He has been fitted with a lightweight compression garment. Ms. N remarked that it seemed to stabilize him posturally, but he protested having it put on and couldn't adjust to wearing it, so the use of it has been discontinued. He is quite big for his age (his height and weight are in the 95th percentile). He is currently in good health.

Background/Behavioral Observation: Ms. N described Neal as a having good verbal skills. He is affectionate with family members and enjoys "hugs and snuggles." He is engaged and has "built good attachments with his caregivers." Neal and his sister are quite involved with each other. He is somewhat interested in and modestly interactive with other children. Both twins attend a Twos Together program twice-weekly for two-hour sessions. Ms. N reported that he enjoys school somewhat (but it is not his favorite thing). Although he reportedly enjoys going to the playground, he remains "close to the ground" all the while, and climbing activities in particular are difficult for him. Neal is also reportedly very sensitive to a range of environmental stimuli. He is also irritable and "cycles quickly from laughing to crying." Neal reportedly has a very difficult time falling asleep at night. In terms of self-care skills Neal can feed himself with utensils. He eats a variety of foods but, as mentioned, will continue to eat until someone stops him. He is not toilet trained yet. He is cooperative with the dressing process but essentially depends on his caregiver to perform most dressing tasks.

I met Neal and his mother in the reception area of the agency office suite and escorted them back to the evaluation room. Neal walked along the hall with a gangly gait. He appeared slightly apprehensive at first but warmed considerably as we played with the fine motor toys and activities. He was friendly and made good eye contact. Neal spoke in full sentences that I found difficult to understand at times due to articulation. He appeared to understand everything that was said to him. He sat at the table for the 30 minutes of fine motor challenges without the need for a movement break of any kind. He understood the task expectations of all of the challenges. There were no dramatic behavioral or emotional over-reactions for the 40 minutes that we all sat and played together.

Gross Motor/Neuromotor Assessment: Neal walked independently at 18 months of age (later than developmentally expected), and commando crawled "for a long time before that."

Active range of motion in all joints is within functional limits.

Muscle tone is low (his muscles feel more flaccid than firm when they are challenged or when resistance is applied).

There are no apparent musculoskeletal asymmetries, contractures, or deformities. There are no dysmorphic facial features.

Arms and legs are proportionate and of equal lengths.

There was no observable evidence of involuntary rapid eye movement that would suggest neurological involvement.

Neal was able to cross his vertical midline during manual task performance.

Neal refused to jump in place, but his mother stated that he makes very tiny jumps at home. He was able to perform a wheelbarrow walking challenge with me supporting his legs, but the task was clearly difficult for him and his shoulder blades were winged (locked in place at the end of their range of motion near his spine, indicating that he could not stabilize his torso muscles without resorting to this compensatory strategy). Neal tends to shy away from physical play.

The **Peabody Developmental Motor Scales-2** is used to assess gross and fine motor skills in children from birth to six years old. The fine motor portion assesses grasp, hand-use, eye–hand coordination, and manual dexterity (the manipulation of small objects by use of the hands).

Fine Motor: Neal was able to pick up slender wooden toy candles one at a time off the table and then insert each one into a corresponding hole in a toy cake. Fingers were conspicuously stiffened as he held each of the slender candles, and he tended to hold his unused hand up with his fingers tensed and curled (a child with poor core strength will deliberately summon tension into their unused hand as a way of experiencing a greater sense of stability, but unfortunately at the expense of individual joint movements). He was able to insert individual coins into a bank slot using good visual direction of the slot to correctly position his wrist. He was able to unscrew the top of a small screw-type jar. Neal was able to tower one-inch blocks ten-high using good visual direction of his hand efforts, but conspicuously thrust his tensed tongue out as he did so (a similar example of tensing an available unused muscle). He was able to replicate the three-dimensional design of a four-block train as would be developmentally expected of a child his age. Neal used an interesting strategy to feed a lace through the hole on a large toy button and then move the button along the length of the string. Rather than holding and feeding the lace with a pincer grasp, he problem solved how to hold the lace against his palm and draped over his hand and then essentially lowered the lace end into the hole. Then, rather than pulling the button along with his fingers, he held the lace up and allowed gravity to pull the button down the length of the string. In this manner he essentially eliminated the need to involve or move his fingers in this two-handed task. He held a crayon in his right hand with an inefficient thumbs-down fisted grip, and kept the crayon nearly level with the paper he was trying to draw on it. In this manner he was able to make wavy and repetitive horizontal and vertical slashes, but not confident, concise lines as I demonstrated for him. Neal initially did not know how to hold scissors but made tiny cuts when they were placed properly in his hand.

Neal's performance, based on the Peabody, resulted in a standard score of 8 (low-average) on the visual-motor subtest, and a 7 (between 1 and 2 standard deviations below age-expected performance) on the grasping subtest.

This results in a fine motor quotient of 85. These scores indicate no remarkable concerns with overall fine motor ability from a developmental perspective. However, it is important to more closely consider the limitations of the test's "developmental" frame of reference. The Peabody awards points when a child is able to accomplish each of the task challenges. However, the test does not look at the kinds of strategies the child employs to accomplish the task, nor does it consider the quality of the task attempt. For example, it does not comment on tensed arm and hand strategies that limit the independent movements of the elbow, wrist, and especially the finger joints. Nor does it subtract points when a child uses compensatory strategies to stabilize their posture, as Neal consistently did with his choice of grips and non-involved hand clenching. Such actions clearly point out the effects of Neal's low tone and postural instability. Until he makes improvements in further strengthening his core muscle groups, he will likely continue to approach fine motor tasks with the same limitations, even as these tasks become increasingly more complex and demanding. Certainly, from a developmental point of view, Neal is clever enough to problem solve and accomplish a number of these task challenges in an inefficient manner. But from a strength/weakness outlook, the quality and efficiency of his execution is conspicuously compromised. In a matter of literally a few more months his current approaches to age-appropriate tasks (that are slightly more sophisticated) will, in my opinion, result in scores that will be notably more concerning.

Sensory Integration: When professional evaluators look at how well a child's sensory systems are working, we are essentially looking at two main areas of potential difficulties, both of which can dramatically affect how a child behaves and matures developmentally. At one extreme is the child who requires an inordinate amount of some kind of sensory input before a sensory experience "registers" with them and allows them to react with an appropriate response. The other extreme describes children who are acutely sensitive to specific types of sensory experiences. Seemingly normal levels of sound, light, smell, or touch may register with them as distracting, uncomfortable, or even distressing.

Based on his mother's responses on the Sensory Profile questionnaire, Neal achieved significantly heightened scores (well into the Definite Difference range) for a Sensation Avoidance behavior profile. This is referred to as a Low Threshold behavior set. A Low Neurological Threshold condition describes a condition in which responses to seemingly benign sensory stimulation are triggered more quickly and dramatically—and therefore frequently— because thresholds are met so easily (a "threshold" refers to the point at which a neurochemical reaction in the brain forces it to respond to a stimulus, similar to a fight or flight response). This is consistent with Ms. N's reports that Neal consistently becomes upset if his face, hands, shoes, or clothing get messy or wet, and will protest having his face washed or wiped, or having lotion applied. He consistently protests grooming activities, especially having his nails trimmed. He has a difficult time being placed on his back onto a cold or rough surface, and rebels at walking barefoot on grass. Neal also startles easily at sound, gets nervous about unfamiliar sounds, and tries to escape from noisy or crowded environments. He is reportedly easily overwhelmed by visually stimulating environments and will frequently cover his eyes (or pull down the shade of his stroller). As mentioned, Neal has a particularly difficult time with rapid movements (such as car rides) or having his head tipped back to shampoo or to be changed. He also reportedly has considerable difficulty in tolerating changes in his routines, and engaging in new activities. Children with hypersensitivity to their environment depend on a familiar and consistent routine as a way of predicting and preparing for what comes into their personal space. As such, transitions are particularly difficult for these children. The Sensory Sensitive child also typically has an especially difficult time in modulating his emotional responses to sensory events that he finds disturbing (modulation refers to a child's ability to react to a sensory stressor with an appropriate and measured emotional response). These children frequently impress others as shy or anxious.

Parents frequently ask what might possibly cause or contribute to persistent and extreme sensitivities in their children. In a great many cases there is a significant correlation between avoidant behaviors and significant histories of digestive complaints/medical insults. Consider the frequent discomfort and pain that must have accompanied many of his treatments as a premie in the clinical environment of the Neonatal Intensive Care Unit for a full month. Add to this his persistent Gastric Reflux symptoms after every feeding for a full year (as well as his repeated bouts of constipation). In very practical terms, consider your own experience with stomach distress or illness, and how reluctant (or loathe) you are during these episodes to participate and try new things, and how even the most benign stimulus can seem unsettling if not threatening. Now extend that to a possible scenario in which these discomforts are longstanding. Such discomfort can eventually permeate one's entire disposition, and inclines the child to approach all but the most secure and familiar settings with apprehension and reluctance.

Summary/Recommendations: Neal is a charming and bright little boy being raised in an obviously caring household. Despite scores in or near the average range in developmental fine motor testing, it is my strong clinical opinion that the quality and efficiency of his movements are seriously compromised by his low muscle tone and diminished core stability. A child's torso muscles must be in a state of readiness and firm enough to provide a stable basis for extremity use without their having to resort to summoning tension into their arms to compensate for this diminished sense of control. Unfortunately this summoned tension limits the relaxed, smooth, and independent finger movements that provide the basis for efficient fine motor practice (basic fine motor skills often do not require much in the way of hand or arm strength, but actually depend on the fingers being relaxed in order to accomplish smooth precision work). Of equal concern, Neal is also conspicuously bothered by heightened and emotionally fraught responses to various sensory stimuli that clearly impact on his comfort levels, limit his willingness to engage in appropriate play, and likely result in his frequent withdrawal from group situations. I am therefore strongly recommending occupational therapy services for Neal at the Committee on Preschool Special Education (CPSE) level at the frequency of two 45-minute sessions a week, preferably in a gym setting that can address his sensory tolerances while also reinforcing his fine motor development and strengthening his core muscles.

WHIT

(A Sensory Indulgent child)

OCCUPATIONAL THERAPY EVALUATION

Name: Whit

Chronological Age: 2 yrs., 11 mos. (35 mos.)

Reason for Referral: Whit is receiving this occupational therapy evaluation as he prepares to age out of the Early Intervention program and to assess sensory-motor functioning and assist in future planning. Primary concerns initially focused on apparent language delays, largely thought to be impacted by significant medically confirmed hearing loss as a younger child, as well as feeding issues. He currently receives the following related services through the Early Intervention program: speech therapy—3 x 30 minutes/week, occupational therapy—3 x 30 minutes/week, physical therapy—1 x 30 minutes/week, and Special Instruction—5 hours/week. The family has recently procured the private services of a Feeding Specialist. Whit is being followed by a holistic developmental pediatrician who takes issue with an Autistic Spectrum Disorder diagnosis given to Whit during the Early Intervention process.

An occupational therapy evaluation will formally evaluate fine motor and visual-motor skills as well as consider whether there are sensory registration, processing, or self-regulation difficulties that could result in atypical behaviors that interfere with developmental gains.

Site of Evaluation: This afternoon evaluation was conducted at the agency office suite. Mrs. W remained with her son throughout the evaluation. We conducted the interview portion of the evaluation by phone several days after the testing. The testing space was appropriate in terms of spaciousness, cleanliness, and relative lack of distraction.

Birth/Medical History/Background: Whit is the only child of Mr. and Mrs. W. Mrs. W reported that her pregnancy was unremarkable following a good course of pre-natal care. Whit was born at full-term. Mrs. W explained that she went into labor 30 hours prior to his delivery, but the contractions were irregular throughout the labor and did not get closer together. Eventually she was administered Pitocin. Whit weighed 7 lbs., 4 oz. at birth. Mrs. W described her son as colicky and very gassy for the first three months of his life (he has since been following a casein-free, soy-free diet designed not to address medical concerns but to expedite development). Mrs. W reported that she became concerned with her son's language development at 18 months of age (he was not using any age-expected vocabulary by that time). His ears were subsequently checked and no blockage was found. However, just six months later significant frustration behaviors apparently related to his language delays resulted in a formal hearing test that determined significant bilateral fluid build-up that was responsible for 100 percent blockage in one ear and up to 60 percent blockage in the other. The initial approach to resolving this issue was to administer low doses of antihistamine. However, Whit developed a negative reaction to the medication, and he eventually underwent an outpatient procedure to implant bilateral tubes in February of 2012. At about the same time Whit was noted to engage in frequent repetitive behaviors, notably opening and closing doors. He developed dramatic responses to electronic devices (specifically to smartphones) and would have "massive tantrums" if a phone should ring and he did not have the chance to answer it in time. He also would not tolerate it when his mother would use the phone. He spoke in jargon, and though reportedly interested in other children, would largely relate only to the adults in the weekly music class he attended. He also demonstrated very little safety awareness on the playground and had poor balance (Mrs. W speculated that this was due to the impact that the fluid blockage imposed on his vestibular mechanisms). Subsequently, Whit was seen by a pediatric neurologist to address the Autistic Spectrum Disorder diagnosis offered by Early Intervention. The physician indicated that it was difficult to confirm or deny the diagnosis in light of Whit's hearing difficulties (in a subsequent consultation with him in August of this year he stated that he did not necessarily think that Whit's behaviors were indicative of an Autistic Spectrum Disorder diagnosis, but that there were clearly important communication issues that needed to be addressed and that these might be responsible for significant interruptions in expected development). In August of this year it became necessary to replace one of the tubes in another procedure, an event that resulted in behavioral setbacks according to Whit's mother and service providers. There have been no additional hospitalizations, serious injuries, or illnesses. There is no significant history of ear infection or ongoing digestive complaints. Mrs. W remarked that there are no pressing concerns with Whit's vision, although he has recently resorted to tilting his head in a stylized manner. Otherwise, Mrs. W described her son as "really healthy."

In terms of self-help skills, Mrs. W reported that Whit has very "low motivation" in terms of feeding himself. He continues to eat only those familiar foods that have been pureed, along with some crunchy food selections. As mentioned, Whit follows a casein-free/soy-free diet that reportedly had an almost immediate positive effect on his behaviors when it was introduced. He is cooperative with dressing and is interested enough to raise his arms to assist putting on a shirt. He is starting to show an interest in toilet training. Whit has "always had other children around him." He makes good eye contact and gets quite attached to certain people. He played with a certain group of children on a regular basis (the children of friends) from the time he was quite young, although he tends to withdraw from group play if more than two other children join in. He enjoys all of the apparatus on the playground. Whit likes to play games such as hide and seek and is reportedly developing some nice pretend play.

Whit's Special Educator described him as "easy to engage." She reported that he is interested in other children and does well with peers. Overall, she stated that his play skills and language has been expanding quite a lot. She further claimed that he had been doing "fantastic" with their work until the setback that accompanied his most recent surgery in August (she commented on his "massive tantrums" that could last for an hour or more). She saw his at-times solitary and repetitive play as a coping mechanism, and added that he is drawn to visually stimulating experiences that have always been sources of considerable comfort and pleasure for him during those times when auditory function was interrupted. She also focused on his strong bias for strong physical input such as spinning, jumping, and crashing. In general she stated that his play skills are still more representative of a younger child, and speculated that his self-soothing strategies have interfered with his development in this area.

Whit's occupational therapist has been working with him for the past "eight or nine months." She recognized that he has both shown progress and suffered some setbacks during that time (she also cited his surgery in this regard). They have been working on improving his registration of vestibular and proprioceptive input, and she also related these issues to his ear insults. Whit was initially quite defensive to tactile events. This has improved over time, but she continues to use a sensory brushing technique during their sessions. She too underscored how Whit takes real comfort in visual stimulation.

Behavioral Observation: Whit was just finishing with his physical therapy evaluation in the agency's sensory gym upon my arrival. He quickly acknowledged my entrance and made unflinching direct eye contact with me for the remainder of our time together. He spoke in a manner that I could not understand (seemingly in jargon), but occasionally would produce a recognizable word (especially when he was singing along with his mother to one of his favorite Willie Nelson songs). His mother claimed that she can understand about 75 percent of what he says to her. He was interested in the toys that I used for the fine motor testing and attempted all of the various task challenges following my visual demonstrations. He remained seated for the 25 minutes of my testing without the need for a major movement break of any kind.

The **Peabody Developmental Motor Scales-2** is used to assess gross and fine motor skills in children from birth to six years old. The fine motor portion assesses grasp, hand-use, eye–hand coordination, and manual dexterity (the manipulation of small objects by use of the hands).

Fine Motor: Whit picked up slender wooden toy candles one at a time using several fingers in somewhat of a chuck-like grip (rather than a neat pincer grip). He was able to insert them into corresponding holes in a toy cake. He was able to pick up coins one at a time off the table surface and attempted to insert each one into a bank slot. However, it was difficult for him at times to correctly orient his wrist position with the alignment of the slot. He was able to remove the top from a small screw-type jar. Whit was able to tower one-inch blocks only six-high (ten-high would be expected for his age). His hand efforts were not visually directed and there was some unsteadiness in his arm as it moved through space. He was also unable to replicate the three-dimensional design of a simple four-block train. Whit was able to feed a lace through the opening of several large plastic buttons, but then could not problem solve how to exchange his hands in order to pull the string through from the other side. He held a crayon with a young, inefficient thumbs-up fisted grasp that insists that the arm, wrist, and fingers move as a fixed unit. He could produce short concise lines following my demonstration, but mostly scribbled on paper. He did not readily anchor the drawing paper with his non-involved hand. Whit did not know how to hold or use scissors on his own.

Based on his demonstrated efforts on standardized testing, Whit's performance resulted in a standard score of 5 (significantly more than two standard deviations below typical age-expected performance) on the visual-motor subtest and a 6 on the grasping subtest of the Peabody.

These represent a fine motor quotient of 73 for overall fine motor skill levels (just shy of two standard deviations below age-expected performance, at only the third percentile, indicating that only 3 percent of children his age achieved scores at this level or lower). These are concerning scores. Overall, Whit's fine motor mannerisms appeared to reflect the impact of diminished core stability, leading him to employ tensed grips and resulting in difficulties relaxing the tension on his wrist and fingers that he recruits to stabilize his hand during tasks. Moreover, his approach to these tasks appears to reflect a general developmental delay in these functional areas. Consistent with this view, his language issues further complicate his learning opportunity and make it necessary for him to rely heavily on visual instruction. This gets further complicated in that these visual detours can often lead to more visually fixating behaviors that change the course of his attention.

Sensory Integration: When professional evaluators look at how well a child's sensory systems are working, we are essentially looking at two main areas of potential difficulties, both of which can dramatically affect how a child behaves and matures developmentally. At one extreme is the child who requires an inordinate amount of some kind of sensory input before a sensory experience "registers" with them and allows them to react with an appropriate response. The other extreme describes children who are acutely sensitive to specific types of sensory experiences. Seemingly normal levels of sound, light, smell, or touch may register with them as distracting, uncomfortable, or even distressing.

Based on his parents' responses on the Sensory Profile questionnaire, Whit achieved significant scores (in the

Definite Difference range) for a Sensation Avoiding behavior profile. This is strongly in evidence in regards to his highly significant Oral Processing scores and his ongoing history of extreme sensitivity to feeding. In addition to these issues, he protests certain grooming practices such as having his nails trimmed and brushing his teeth (another oral experience). He is also "keenly aware" of when his clothing, hands, and face get messy. Whit's behavior also reportedly significantly deteriorates when changes are introduced into his routines and schedules (the Sensory Avoidant child does everything they can to ensure that routines remain constant and predictable rather than allow for the possibility of some novel or unexpected stimulus that might prove discomforting). Now that his hearing is restored he is also highly distracted by sound and will frequently cover his ears when sound levels increase. It is perhaps interesting to note that I have worked with young children who have had their hearing restored with the use of hearing aids, but frequently choose to turn the device off on their own because the hearing experience can be startling and uncomfortable for them at times (compared with the insulated non-hearing experience that they can remember).

Attention should also be paid to Whit's intentional diversion to visually stimulating events that has at times intruded on his development. The Sensory Profile is credited with creating a paradigm that classifies children this age into one of four behavior categories. However, it does not categorically acknowledge the persistent actions of the child who might be referred to as "Sensory Indulgent." Children who perseverate on spinning, shiny, or textural objects are often misunderstood to be Sensory Seeking. The "Seeking" child is actually a child who prioritizes rich and strong sensory input to compensate for an otherwise dull experience due to the stimulus being inefficiently processed in the brain. The Sensory Indulgent child is more closely related to the Highly Sensitive child (consistent with Whit's scores on the Profile). We often make the erroneous assumption that the hypersensitive child's sensory issues are invariably recognized by and related to their discomfort levels with tolerating certain trigger events. However, the Highly Sensitive child can also be seen as having a much more heightened experience of comfort and pleasure as they process certain stimuli. Visual stimulation can be among the most powerful and meaningful of these attractions. In one sense this sounds quite compelling. However, these distractions can often divert a child's attention to the exclusion of other meaningful learning and social opportunities. It seems somewhat clear that Whit struggles both with certain aspects of the discomfort produced by these hypersensitivities, as well as with the significant, but distracting, comfort practices that he has learned to identify in his visual experience. Both aspects of these sensitivities have the potential to seriously interrupt typical development.

Summary/Recommendations: Whit is a curious and social young boy being raised in a caring household. Standardized scores on fine motor testing indicate significant delays in fine motor abilities (approximately two standard deviations below age-expected performance—at the third percentile for his age group). This appears to reflect a significant delay in development in this functional area. Fine motor approaches are also likely impacted by his diminished core stability. Scores on sensory testing point out significantly heightened sensitivities to oral, auditory, and vestibular events, but also are likely responsible for his reverting to comfort and pleasure practices that he compellingly engages in to the exclusion of more appropriate and meaningful learning events. Although the Sensory Profile scoring does not recognize it, Whit is also frequently biased towards strong physical and vestibular input.

I am therefore strongly recommending that occupational therapy services should continue in place for Whit at the Committee on Preschool Special Education (CPSE) level in a gym setting that can address his fine motor development, sensory registration challenges, and core strength issues.

THE SELF-REGULATION PIECE AND BOTH ENDS OF THE CONTINUUM

For a few days every February at my home in Upstate New York, the outside temperature predictably reaches 30 degrees below zero—a sharp contrast to those humid mid-90 degree days we plod through in late July. Despite these uncomfortable extremes, most of us can accept the situation, prepare ourselves mentally, pull our pants on, and drive to work in the morning. We're able to do so by making accommodations to the weather—putting on extra clothes, caps, mittens, and heavy socks, or staying close to the air-conditioning. Obviously, these are scenarios that insist that our brains defend us by resisting these extreme insults of temperature. But as we have learned from both the High Threshold and Low Threshold child, our efforts to resist or actively compensate for the sensory information that tries to register are sometimes not enough. These compensations can create their own set of concerns and miseries. There's another thing that we depend on to see us through the challenges our sensory environment faces us with that also has to kick in, and kick in fast. This is the self-regulation piece that you may have heard about. At almost the same time that the brain has to recognize what a sensory message represents, and then do its best to either help it along (such as the Sensory Seeking child) or offer it some resistance (such as the Sensory Defensive child), it should also come up with an immediate, tailored, and somewhat appropriate response for the situation in which it occurs. As if the work of the sensory child isn't difficult enough, learning platforms and socialization values insist that the child somehow insinuate judgment in between the trigger event and the typically more aggravated response that they are prepared to offer. Some of this depends on a child's developmental level—that is, their level of social, physical, and emotional maturity. Some of it involves educational agendas. Children are supposed to be taught appropriate socialization strategies by their parents and teachers. All of it involves the hard work that the sensory child must do to get back to the comfort zone that we talked about much earlier. These children first require that these issues be properly identified. For all of the chatter, Sensory Processing is still the new kid on the block, and not everyone still understands it when it speaks. Then in many cases it requires support services to help these children re-experience their feelings in a more structured and hopefully more effective manner. Moving closer to the center along the sensory continuum is the goal.

One last set of comments... Over the course of my career I have met children who are the classic presentation of each of these sensory behavior patterns. I have repeatedly met the Sensory Seeking child, the Sensory Defensive child, the Under-Responsive child, and the Sensory Sensitive child. But these categories are just constructs that help us make sense of a child's major issues. More often than not, such children do not display every behavior that I have associated with each of the processing disorders. People simply do not fit precisely into categories. Usually there is enough compelling evidence based on these models that a trained evaluator recognizes each respective member of this sensory family. It then becomes a matter of determining whether these behavioral presentations are significant enough to interfere with the child's life roles—student, playmate, family member. It is only when the involved parties reach that consensus that we recognize these children as having a dysfunction.

But there are other children—many of them—who display both significantly High and Low Threshold behaviors. At first this appears to be a contradiction. How can a child be highly unmotivated to respond to some aspects of their environment while also hypersensitive to other aspects? Some of the answer has to do with the separate nerve pathways that relay this information to the brain. If you own an old house you realize that some of the electrical circuits are not always dependable. Similarly, these separate sensory paths and the chemical reactions that distinguish them are not equally efficient. I liken it to a road map. If you plot your approach to your destination, you notice that there are superhighways, commercial roads, the old blue highways that aren't used as much anymore, and some thin wavy black lines on the map that promise to take you where you're going, but you can assume that it will be slow, arduous and rough-going. They all go to the same place, but the speed and efficiency of the road will determine how quickly and safely you get there. I can't say it any better than I did earlier. Each different type of sensory receptor is hooked up to the brain by way of specific, dedicated nerve pathways, like freight cars traveling on a certain train track that only carry a specific product like corn syrup or coal. One carries auditory, another visual, still others tactile, and so on. Therefore, there is not much of a contradiction that some children are peculiarly sensitive to some things, and nearly oblivious to others.

The composite that emerges describes a child who on the one hand struggles to find ways to greatly enhance certain sensory input to meet comfort thresholds, while on the other hand cannot tolerate a range of stimuli that does manage to register.

CHAPTER 3

A CAUTIONARY TALE...

It seems that not a month goes by during the school year when someone on the staff doesn't approach me with their concerned appraisal of a student. Most vividly, for example, I remember the cashier at the end of the cafeteria line who lowered her usual uplifting, pleasant voice, looked me square in the eyes, and instructed me: "You've got to do something about David. He's got sensory issues." One way of looking at this is that people are paying attention to recent trends in education, and that the topic of Sensory Processing Disorder has firmly made its way into the vocabulary. The bigger statement, of course, is that the whole notion of Sensory Processing Disorder seems to have gone viral, and that many well-intentioned people already feel that they understand its premises well enough to make such casual assessments. To be sure there are those educators who are interested enough in this fairly complicated territory to take additional professional development classes in the subject, or at least ask the right questions of the right people before they start passing judgment. But the truly impressive thing to emerge from these exchanges is the comfort and ease with which non-professionals share their critical opinion about this specific topic. None of these people are stopping me in the halls to tell me that Suzie's behaviors are consistent with a child who is on the Autistic Spectrum, or that Xavier's activity level and impulsivity are clearly the presentations of a child with Attention Deficit/Hyperactivity Disorder (ADHD), or that sweet little Emily who is so squeamish and isolating in class is suffering from an anxiety disorder. Those designations are clearly still off-limits for anyone who is not a physician or a psychologist. And in fact, these are the rules. These last-mentioned diagnoses are given to children exclusively by trained experts who draw them from carefully detailed lists of criteria in the *Diagnostic and Statistical Manual of Mental Disorders* (the "DSM," now in its fifth edition). For years this publication has been considered the international authority for all kinds of brain disorders in children and adults.

A diagnosis of Sensory Processing Disorder, despite intense lobbying efforts, does not appear in the DSM-5. It is a designation developed by and usually given by an occupational therapist who has invested some considerable time and study to understand its complexities, and learned how to plan a hopefully effective treatment program for the right children. This does not mean that the broad range of concerns that define a Sensory Processing Disorder is refuted or overlooked by the established medical community. Sensory problems are, for example, on the list of qualifying symptoms for a diagnosis of Autistic Spectrum Disorder (ASD) in the DSM-5. But this is delicate terrain. Sensory treatments might in fact be used with these other children, and may in some cases bring out their most positive and developmentally appropriate interactions with their school environment. However, this does not mean that every child with sensory processing inefficiencies is on the Spectrum. There are, to be sure, many young children who do not qualify for a formal diagnosis of ASD, or for that matter ADHD, Developmental Delay, Emotionally Disturbed, and so on, whose learning opportunities and behaviors are made problematic by their inefficient response to their sensory environment. These are the classic sensory kids. The overall clinical community largely agrees with that, and most school systems are prepared to award related support services to such a child when a persuasive case can be made by an occupational therapist that convincingly states that just these problems are significantly challenging the child's ability to function in their role as "student." But it can get confusing.

There are two important points to be made following such a discussion. First, it is so important to get an accurate understanding of a child's problems. Competent evaluation and the conclusions drawn from that should skillfully discriminate among the many similar symptoms of key childhood disorders. The correct determination guides the correct treatment and consequently delivers the best outcomes. To put this in strong sensory language, not every hyperactive child is a Sensory Seeker, not every isolating child is a Sensory Defensive—which leads to my second point. A designation of Sensory Processing Disorder can be seductive, especially to parents. It seems to lack the decisiveness and the severity of some of these other disorders that may have entered into the conversation. It does not come with a prescription drug plan that can otherwise be so loathsome to parents. It appears, to many outward appearances, to be "diagnosis lite." It lacks both the punch and the stigma that accompany many other maladies. It can be taken advantage of to hide behind, both emotionally and socially.

What am I driving at? Just this. When you begin this arduous and often painful process of recruiting a professional to help you better understand your child's problems, first consider all the possibilities that are raised from others' informed input. Then look at your personal observations of your child's behavior squarely in the face. But don't stop short of listening to more troubling opinions just because sensory processing is a safer respite. Use your best, most honest instincts in moving forward. Finally, remind yourself that even though all of us have our own sensory quirks, it's only when they seriously interfere with development or function that they demand attention and help. Keep in mind that, when they do, the impact of real sensory issues can be just as intrusive as many of these other conditions.

CHAPTER 4

FINALLY...

Some closing comments...

One of the questions I am asked the most is "Will my child outgrow this?" Will these children continue to struggle with environments that they find too distressing, or persist in behaviors aimed at dramatically accentuating their contact with their world? Despite my efforts to research this, there is simply not a lot written about how a young sensory child's status changes in later childhood and even into their adult years. There are some compelling entries on the Internet from adults who confess to have suffered from extreme Sensory Defensiveness throughout their lives—often as a result of being misdiagnosed or ignored (remember, kids used to be dismissed with one-word diagnoses such as "fussy," "hyper," "dull," etc.). Those who have never had these issues professionally addressed still tell very moving stories about the extreme accommodations and compromises they are forced to make in order to function as an adult, and get any joy from their world. These are likely extreme cases, far from the center of the comfort zone continuum.

This is what I'm fairly confident of. I work primarily with children up to the age of six years old (I have also spent a considerable amount of time working with elementary school children). At these young ages, various developmental abilities may mature at different rates. The functional skill that pushes its way to the front of the line is our ability to use and understand language appropriately. Children whose receptive and expressive speech is behind schedule have a considerably more difficult time getting their needs met. They cannot adequately describe situations and events that they find distressing, nor can they explain their insistent need for movement breaks throughout their day. Communication skills, when they become more readily available to children, provide them with significantly more options for them to be accommodated, and as such these issues may seem to have abated. The more accurate statement, however, is that these issues have not gone away. They are simply easier to recognize and address (thus relieving some of the stress).

That's not to say that all sensory kids are faced with a life sentence. Mother Nature helps a lot. I'm convinced that some children actually do physically mature out of these extreme zones. I'm reminded that some children are not potty trained until four or five years of age, largely because their little bodies can't properly interpret those signals that tell them their bladder is full or they need to poop. At some point, their physical development just begins to make sense of it, perhaps with the added reinforcement of social expectations. Some of our sensory children eventually reach a point where their brains are better able to recognize what these various signals mean, and whether they represent any kind of real threat. The quality of their life may also be improved if a co-existing medical condition that exacerbates their sensory status has been brought under control.

Here's the bottom line: I believe that all of us develop a sensory signature quite early in life, either before or soon after we are born. My strong opinion is that we carry this predisposition with us throughout the remainder of our years. As in my own story, I did not at first fully recognize why I was predisposed to react in predictable ways to everyday occurrences, and why I comfort myself with certain dependable routines. Knowing what I do now, such actions are perfectly consistent with the way I've approached my sensory world since I was a child. Remember, we all react to our sensory world in a unique way. And we all make accommodations and compromises with respect to those dispositions, hopefully simple ones (sandals on or off at the beach, radio on or off while you read, and so forth). But it's at this point that we must remind ourselves about our more immediate concerns—our children's day-to-day comfort levels and preparedness to learn.

The world of parents with babies or young children with Sensory Processing Disorders can be a pressure cooker. It can start with an infant who cannot be consoled, or reacts furiously to being held. Perhaps it's the baby who doesn't make eye contact or doesn't make any of those lovely babbling sounds, and just sort of lays there. Maybe it's the toddler who needs to be watched at all times to ensure they don't deliberately crash into furniture and walls or jump from a stair landing and hurt themselves. What about the child who needs to be wrestled and pinned down just to be dressed (not to mention the nightmare of haircuts, visits to the dentist, and having their nails trimmed)? These are the years that Sensory Processing Disorders can be at their fever pitch. We wouldn't be content to patiently wait for the next six years for our flu symptoms to pass if someone reassured us that they would improve by then. These issues need to be respected and addressed now. Of course it's difficult for all your family members to get through some of these recurring episodes. But be sure to shift your primary focus to what your child is experiencing. They are the ones to whom it is happening first and most forcefully.

Help is available. Well-trained therapists can now offer interventions that have proven significantly effective in bringing these children closer to the center of that comfort zone, hopefully using activities that these kids find motivating and fun. Very low tolerances to certain aspects of their environment can be sensitively and gradually raised. Very poor registration can be worked with until a child better recognizes what their bodies are supposed to feel, thus allowing them to better attend to their world and react accordingly. But the first step is to recognize and understand what your child is going through. Be persistent but open minded, well informed but not a know-it-all. Ask realistic questions about your child and wait for answers that you understand. Renew your commitment to this undertaking and revive your patience at the beginning of each new day. Keep a daily journal to better understand your child's successes and challenges. Remain involved firsthand. As a better informed parent you have an amazing potential to influence the outcome. Most of all, enjoy these special years with your children. They truly are one-of-a-kind marvels. Laughter and smiles grace just about every childhood, at times more often than we realize.

SPECIAL ACKNOWLEDGMENT

"It moves!" Galileo is reputed to have whispered defiantly after being forced by the Inquisitors to publicly retract his scientific theory that the earth revolved around the sun, and not the other way around. Despite his captors' brief victory, the force and clarity of his science prevailed, and his ideas reshaped the way we understand our cosmos and define ourselves as human beings. Occupational therapists and educators consider the work of A. Jean Ayres just as revolutionary. Her vision of the profound impact of our sensory system's connection to the world around us brought a previously invisible world view into crisp focus. We are all in her debt for first recognizing and then writing about the science of Sensory Integration.

Some 20 years ago, as I was working towards my degree, occupational therapy programs were just starting to discuss Sensory Integration. My own course work covered the topic in one 45-minute class, and then didn't look back. It wasn't until I was in the workplace and came across a new standardized evaluation instrument called the Sensory Profile by Winnie Dunn that I was able to grasp what this model really meant, even after several years of professional practice, continuing education, and discussion with colleagues. And now, as with all good science that is reviewed and challenged, the discussion continues, drawing from many different points of view. I hope that my perspective makes these tall concepts that much more accessible to those it impacts on the most— the parents and teachers of small children wrestling with sensory issues.

AN OT'S SUGGESTIONS FOR
THE PRE-SCHOOL CLASSROOM

The traditional role of the Preschool Occupational Therapist (OT) is to work with fine motor and visual-motor difficulties (grasp, manipulation of small objects, use of both hands, motor planning and execution, body awareness, eye–hand coordination) as they impact on pre-academic learning readiness and self-care routines. Over the last few decades, we have also been called on to consider whether there are sensory registration, processing, or self-regulation difficulties responsible for considerable discomfort, or behaviors that interfere with typical developmental gains or school preparedness. Persistent actions such as attention difficulties, heightened activity levels, and non-participation in group activities (either because the child is aloof and chooses to remain on the group periphery, or because the child is determined to follow their own agenda) may *in some cases* be the result of the child's diminished ability to interact with their sensory environment (obviously there can be other causes and explanations for some of these behaviors).

The most familiar intervention pursued by a Therapist is to work directly with a child suspected of having classroom difficulties such as those mentioned above. However, the OT frequently finds it helpful and necessary to make adjustments to the classroom environment itself or to the child's routine.

These strategies can make a significant difference in how well the child can adjust to the long school day that they spend with you. Some children require someone on the teaching staff to follow through with a Therapist's recommendations on a daily basis. In other cases minor adjustments to the classroom lay-out or minor tweaks to the daily routine can make an otherwise difficult day more successful for everyone. At other times sensory nuisances that may seem benign to most children can have a frightful effect on certain little ones. Noise levels, lighting levels, and room temperature can have a dramatically different impact on the hypersensitive child, and their responses may be mistaken for different inappropriate behaviors. There can be common-sense adjustments that can sometimes improve on these situations.

During my career I have learned some great ideas from speaking with experienced teachers. Some of the advice is very general and involves no cost. Some ideas require modest purchases that could make a big difference. Much of it is trial and error. Always keep in mind that the strategy that meets with little success at first may yet be helpful if given a chance over a period of time.

Remember, if there is only one idea that you walk away with, then the effort has been worthwhile.

FINE MOTOR

WRITING PROBLEMS AND PRACTICE SUGGESTIONS

1. Seize every opportunity to have a child draw or write. One of your first opportunities of the day is to have a sign-in sheet. This can be prepared at the beginning of the school year for every child in your class, and then Xeroxed in order to have new sheets for every day. The sheet can have the child's picture inserted at the top of the page with their first name in large bold letters. Underneath this would be lined paper like a sheet of primary school writing paper. Depending on the child's ability level you can prepare this so that the name is reprinted on one of these lines, but in dotted-line format for the child to trace along. Below this space I would also suggest inserting a vertical line, a horizontal line, a circle, an intersecting cross, and a square in dotted line format that they can also trace over. Do as much or as little of this sheet over the course of your morning, using hand-over-hand help if necessary (or have the child's parent or caretaker help them without actually doing it for them).

2. In days gone by every child's desktop was tilted at about a 45 degree angle —for a good reason. Efficient writing practice calls for the wrist to be extended slightly (pushing the hand slightly back). In general it also discourages a child from holding a crayon or pencil in a fisted grip or with their hand pushed forward as much as possible in a locked position. Obviously you can't run out and buy new desks for all the children who are struggling with this. But you can fairly easily make a slant board (or buy an inexpensive one) for the child who persists in hooking their hand position forward.

This was also the reason for blackboards in every classroom (upright writing surfaces insist that the hand be pushed back). Since most classes don't have them anymore, try to introduce a good-sized chalkboard that can be leaned against a wall for some of your activities (Circle Time is a good opportunity). If a chalkboard is beyond your reach then try to get an easel—and use it.

Desk and chair heights are also critically important during early drawing and writing practice. If a child's feet don't reach the floor then they do not have a stable base that allows them to free up their upper extremity use for writing. Similarly, if the desk top is so high that the child has to lift their arms (straight out to the side) to rest their elbows on the desk, then their handwriting efforts are compromised. Some desks are adjustable, many are not. The ideal posture for such activities is feet at 90 degrees on the floor, knees at 90 degrees, straight back, and arms mostly down with the desk top two inches higher than their elbows when held against the sides of their body (90–90–90). If the furniture is not adjustable then you may need to introduce steps for their feet to reach the floor. And perhaps a large phone book or an old dictionary on the seat to raise their body to where their elbows are not up in the air.

3. Pencil/crayon grip is often the single most conspicuous clue that the child cannot adequately control the utensil. From the age of about 3 1/2 we expect a child to hold a crayon with a pinch grip, much like an adult's. The child who uses a tense fisted grip with all their fingers wrapped along the shaft—either with their thumb pointed down or pointing up (an even younger and less efficient grip)—cannot move their fingers. Efficient writing practice starts with being able to independently move our fingers back and forth as our hand remains stable. Don't wait until the child is 3 1/2 to try to start changing their grip.

There are a bunch of different grip adapters to try to encourage the correct placement of the fingers. Kids are amazing in their ability to ignore these adapters and still grab the pencil in their fist. One thing to try with more encouraging results is to use short crayons (about 2 inches long). It's difficult to hold a short crayon in a fist. Nice short crayons are commercially available, or you can buy a set of Large Crayolas (not the Jumbos or the triangular ones) and then neatly shorten them with a razor blade. The important thing is to make these special crayons (or pencils) consistently available to the child who needs help. I've worked in classrooms where the teacher has replaced all the crayons in the classroom with such short crayons so that everyone benefits and there is no chance of lapsing into the bad habits described above.

There are several more promising adapters. One looks like a wishbone and has the child rests their index finger in the Y while holding the shaft with their thumb and other fingers. Another idea is to get a ping pong ball and take the time to drill a hole in it for a pencil shaft to pass through it. This helps support the arch in the hand that is so difficult for certain weak hand grips to fashion and maintain, and doesn't tire the hand so quickly. There are also lightweight spandex gauntlets that can be slipped over the child's hand and wrist while leaving the fingers free. These do a great job for some low-tone children who need additional but comfortable support and hand stability. Still another strategy is to take a small lightweight sock and cut two holes in the toe area, one for the thumb and the other for the index finger to poke through, thus giving the child little choice but to experiment with a pinch grip on the utensil.

4. Many handwriting/drawing difficulties are simply the result of hand weakness. The classic OT activity to improve hand strength is to embed small objects (pennies, bingo chips, buttons) in a wad of light or medium resistant Theraputty and have the child dig them out with their fingers. This can get boring pretty quick, so I recommend that you look for more interesting manipulatives to hide in the putty (I like to use a set of old metal Monopoly game pieces). Of course, it's always important to carefully monitor the child who puts things in their mouth. Another helpful product is a small hand and finger exerciser made by a company called VIA. This fits in the palm and has four push down pistons, much like the valves on a trumpet. They can be purchased in different degrees of resistance (ultra-lite, extra-lite, lite, and so on) to fit the special needs of each child. These also make a good hand fidget toy. Other hand strengthening activities include lacing beads and inserting coins in a bank (especially if the child has to hold four or five coins in their hand at the same time and maneuver just one coin to put in the slot). Any activity that involves isolating the index finger for use in a pincer grip is helpful.

CUTTING DIFFICULTIES

One of the reasons why a child's scissors skills are delayed is simply their lack of experience. Many parents are afraid to let their children use scissors. And yet, our developmental charts tell us that a 25-month-old child should be able to hold appropriate scissors correctly and independently open and close the blades to snip along the edge of paper. By 37 months the child should be able to smoothly cut the paper in half. By 42 months they should be able to cut within 1/4 inch of a pre-drawn straight vertical line the length of the paper. By 50 months they should be able to cut out the periphery of a 3" diameter circle within 1/4 inch of the line.

One of the biggest problems with being able to perform some of these feats is the position of the wrist. Scissors need to be held with the thumb pointing upwards. Similarly, the other hand holding the paper should also have the thumb pointed up. One way to encourage this is to buy one of those large foam thumbs-up signs (notorious at football games) to give them a visual cue and reminder of what position to use. I always get a kick when I ask young children to give me the thumbs-up sign, only to have them stick their index finger in the air. Practicing the right thumbs-up sign throughout the day is a good way of preparing for cutting and finger isolation in general.

SENSORY KIDS

This covers an awful lot of ground, as not all sensory difficulties as they are typically identified by classroom staff are caused by the same set of influences.

What you need to know is that sensory problems often manifest themselves as persistent learning difficulties, socialization issues, and/or "behavioral" problems.

There are essentially four subsets in the Sensory "family"—terms that you are probably familiar with. The first two are related in that their actions and responses are those of a child who does not fully process certain types of sensory information and therefore have an incomplete, unsatisfying experience (of auditory, visual, movement, weight-bearing, or a combination of several). These two children are labeled either Low Registration kids or Sensory Seeking kids.

The Low Registration child simply has little motivation to do anything to activate their alert system. These children present with a low affectation, are usually quite sedentary, and simply do not efficiently register what's going on around them. They typically have very poor body awareness.

Everybody seems to know the Sensory Seeking child. These are the bangers and crashers—the kids who are in constant motion and need to be in constant contact with objects, people, and surfaces. They are pushers and jumpers and twirlers (which can get them in trouble on occasion). They too have a poor sense of their body and personal space (their own and that of others). These are the kids who hug others too tightly or kneel on their chair seat—anything to strongly enhance the experience that is otherwise somewhat dull and certainly preoccupying for them (in much the same way that we can think of little else when our leg falls asleep and we choose to stomp on it until our comfort level is restored). These children are constantly scanning their immediate environment for more powerful opportunities of pressure, resistance, and impact, and are often seen as inattentive or uncooperative in the process. They may not be able to sit through a Circle Time or stay with an activity very long at all.

On the other side of the Sensory continuum are two other related clans of the Sensory family. Both have extremely heightened responses to certain stimuli because it takes very little sound, light, touch, or movement before their brain is forced to respond to the trigger event. These are the Sensory Sensitive child and the Sensory Averse child. Simply stated, the Sensory Sensitive child cannot protect themselves against the deluge of sensory events that happen throughout their day. They have not learned how to rule out certain signals as redundant and unimportant, and therefore respond to mostly everything as though experiencing it for the first time. Their heads are on a swivel. The Sensory Averse child, on the other hand, is uncomfortable or even distressed to the point where they choose to adamantly protect themselves from unpleasant events (that might not otherwise bother most of us). They are vigilant, remain on the periphery of a group, and adhere to exact routines that they know to be predictable. They are the protesters who cannot tolerate getting even slightly messy or handle messy art materials. Although capable of being comfortable and enjoying themselves, they need considerable reassurance that a situation is non-threatening before they can relax. Birthday parties, movies, and concerts can be a nightmare.

With all this in mind, let's turn to the sensory behaviors that typically arise in the classroom.

Perhaps the most frequent report I hear about from a teacher who has singled out a child for a referral is that the child can't sit still during a group activity on the carpet. This child squirms, fidgets, and repositions themselves frequently into different postural positions (from kneeling to sprawling full-out on the rug, to curling up into a tight ball). This child's body is in constant motion, swaying, leaning, and pressing on the floor. This child may also regularly attempt to leave the group to pursue their own agenda, and may even attempt to leave the room. Sometimes limited classroom staff and classroom management in general is actually better served by allowing this child to get away with such behaviors until a better solution is arrived at. Obviously their attention is not trained on the activity in progress and the teachers cannot spend all of their time attempting to redirect just one child.

It is important to note from the outset of these kinds of behaviors how the child occupies themselves once they have left the group. If the child merely drifts from one part of the classroom to another, perhaps gravitating to where their favorite toy is, then these are not likely sensory-influenced behaviors and may not respond to sensory strategies. The same is true for the child who simply moves along to examine things for a very short time before moving on to another spot, *and* their activity level is not particularly boisterous (many such kids move calmly from one place to another and just can't seem to settle). Not all attention and focus issues are sensory in origin. The child who is truly motivated to seek additional sensory input through more powerful physical challenges (thus earning them the designation of being a Sensory Seeker) will be conspicuous as they find ways to engage their body in noticeably more physical play while moving about. They may climb on tables, push against bookcases, or bang toys on the table during that effort. It is quite common for such a child to have something in their hand at all times.

It is extremely important to consider other reasons why such a child will follow their own agenda during Group. The first thing to consider is the child's language ability. Does the child use and understand language enough for their interest to be maintained by a primarily language-focused activity such as Circle Time or having a story read by the teacher? Obviously if the child does not understand some, much, or any of what the teacher is saying then their attention and cooperation will be extremely challenged. What would your day be like if you had to sit and listen to someone who you didn't understand all day long? I have frequently watched such children who will sit with a vague detached expression on their face as the teacher reads a story or asks questions, often not even looking in the appropriate direction, only to have their attention snapped back into place as soon as a movement or music or dance exercise is introduced into the group agenda. This they can understand and respond to.

Keep in mind that a child's language facility may not serve them well for a number of reasons. Many of our children are raised in families in which English is a second language, or not spoken at all. Or perhaps they have a functional grasp of English but can only understand it when their parents speak it (and not when the teacher speaks with an entirely different accent). Other children may have receptive speech difficulties. Still others may simply be developmentally off schedule (you wouldn't expect a two-year-old to sit through a sedentary 15-minute floor activity). As frustrating as this may be for everyone, one simply can't expect the immature preschooler to perform beyond their developmental capacity. *You need to vary your expectations based on the developmental level of each child*. Developmental calendars that describe typical behaviors and abilities at almost monthly increments of age are readily available on the internet. It's often quite telling to plot your child's aptitudes on these charts.

Before listing strategies that might help the Sensory Seeking child, it's important to emphasize the importance of regular movement and physical work opportunities during the course of a typical preschool day. Even some of the nicest preschools do not have dedicated spaces, gyms, or indoor playgrounds that are available to their students on a daily basis. Most classes are brought to nearby outdoor playgrounds, but this is obviously contingent on nice weather. In the meantime, kids need to move and use their muscles for a few reasons. First, to activate their alert systems so that they are better prepared to engage with teachers, classmates, and their learning preparedness. This is especially true first thing in the morning. Second, to strengthen and stabilize their bodies. And third, to address the significant sensory cravings of certain children who may otherwise be entirely disruptive. It's also important at this point to distinguish between free play (that can switch on some children's alert systems, but may lead to other children becoming further unregulated), simple breathing and stretching exercises such as yoga (a good way to start the day), and heavy work experiences that send convincing (and sometimes calming) messages to a child's muscles. The right kind of exercise at the right time can make a big difference on the rest of the child's school day.

So let's consider the simple strategies you can try to help the restless child through a Circle Time. I'll start with suggestions that may require little or no expense.

First, if it does not completely disturb the room arrangement you had in mind for a good reason, hold your group activity in the far corner of the room, and face all the children towards the corner to reduce the possibility of distractions. If it's possible, have the wall spaces behind where you sit as uncluttered and undecorated as possible. Visualize a place that makes you feel comfortable and use that idea to guide how you decorate. If you're not particularly good at this sort of thing, ask another teacher who has a knack for it to help you. There's nothing wrong with introducing pillows and even curtains if they help.

Find some way to partition off this space at least partially. Use bookcases, storage units, file cabinets, or some other physical barrier that helps to keep these children in this dedicated space (while still leaving an entrance space of course). The Circle Time space that simply opens up at the back is an invitation for some kids to just get up and walk away. I know of some classrooms that have gone so far as to introduce an archway or trellis at the entrance to this space. The restless child can also use these physical boundaries to lean up against for more heightened physical feedback, exactly what they crave.

Try to keep the environment as natural as possible. See if there's enough natural light without those intense and sometimes agitating fluorescent fixtures. Keep the window partially open if possible to let some fresh air in. Bring in some plants, or better yet have each child grow a plant from seed and tend to it at a certain point in the day.

Assign each child a definite place to sit on the carpet. This is perhaps best done with colored plastic circles. Take that one more step and either laminate or tape their name to a specific circle or a photograph of each. Children aren't always listening to instructions to sit on a certain colored square. A picture makes it theirs. These circles should be positioned a full arm's length from each other—an exercise that you can have your students perform at the beginning of the activity by holding one arm out to their right side until it touches the shoulder of their neighbor. Separate children who you know are likely to distract each other. Place the most uncooperative student right at your side where you can give them modest tactile cues to help them.

Have seat cushions available for the especially restless child. These can be rubber cushions partially inflated with air or they can be vibrating (you'll need to use rechargeable batteries with these as they run down fairly quickly). Still other cushions are partly filled with air and also have safe rubber-coated marbles inside that give the fidgety child even more pronounced input. These are all trial and error suggestions. If a child does not respond to them, they may require a weighted lap blanket (there are instructions about how to make these online, but they can certainly also be purchased through sensory catalogs). Variations on the lap blanket are weighted shoulder wraps that drape over the child's shoulders. Some children may require even stronger input such as a weighted vest or a compression vest. Obviously these sorts of articles require a therapist to design a schedule for wearing one (most cannot just be left on all day).

Hand fidgets will often give a child something to occupy their hands with as they sit through a group. There are many variations of these. Some are simply small rubber balls. Other are filled with air or pasty substances that allow the child to squeeze the ball until it bulges out. A real low-tech possibility is to give a child a few rubber bands or even some sticky masking tape to play with.

As mentioned, start a Circle Time with some simple yoga stretches, and by doing so perhaps save the Seeking child the effort of finding such opportunities on their own outside the group.

Use a visual icon schedule throughout the day, but especially as children transition into a group activity and as the activity unfolds, to assist language or auditory challenged children. These are plentifully available online for free (try Boardmaker.com). I think it's a good idea to also display a written label alongside each picture that tells them what they're supposed to be focusing on. In general mostly everything in the classroom should have a picture and a label displayed near it.

Such schedules can also be personalized for individual students. They can take their photograph from a poster (attached by velcro) and place it somewhere on a pictorial menu of classroom centers or routines before they are allowed to proceed with the next activity.

If you have a digital camera, use it daily during Circle Time to catch someone being good, and then show the class those pictures on a computer screen or smartboard at the end of the group. Seeing your picture can be a good motivator for good behaviors if its done on a regular basis.

MOVEMENT OPTIONS

As discussed, not all preschools have adequate or equipped spaces for children to use their bodies in. That leaves it up to the teaching staff to be creative in terms of introducing movement. That being said, the catalog of human movements is rather limited. Walk, run, skip, gallop, jump, roll, kneel, spin, balance, stretch on tiptoes, dance—that's most of it. Find ways to incorporate some of these in a classroom movement session. These are perhaps most enticing when incorporated into a game or activity (rather than just allowing a child to jump, have them jump while other children sing part of a song and then give someone else a turn).

Perhaps the easiest way to do that is with music. Kids learn songs quickly, and if there is a movement component involved they learn even quicker. There are some wonderful participation songs for children out there.

In addition, a teacher can find time to lead the children through a classroom space or into the halls with a dance line with each child holding on to the hips of the child in front of them as the music plays. Then there are old standards such as London Bridge (with two children selected to be the bridge as the other children pass under their arched, raised arms), the limbo, and musical chairs. New songs by artists such as Steve and Greg are wonderful for drawing children in.

Sometimes such simple, non-taxing movement opportunities are not enough for a truly sensory kid. They need supervised invitations to engage in supervised "heavy work." You may have heard suggestions to have this child do wall push-ups by simply facing a wall and pushing against it as hard as possible. Introduce some imagination into it to sustain their interest. Tell them that the school bus is stuck in the mud and that they have to push it out (how about getting really daring and doing a mural of the back of the bus on one wall?). You can also assign the Seeking child to be responsible for taking chairs off the tables at the start of the day and putting them back up at the end of the day if it makes sense schedule-wise.

Have a wagon or a toy shopping cart that you can fill with heavy dictionaries, encyclopedias, and books. Ask your sensory child to deliver it to the next classroom (it needs to be heavy enough for them to have to work to move it, but not so heavy that they can't move it at all). Once they arrive at the other classroom, have that teacher prepared to take some books out and replace them with other heavy books to return to their classroom. You might even want to give this child a special hat or a badge that designates their important status as a courier.

If the wagon idea is not an option then fill a small bookbag with similar heavy books. Make sure the bookbag is strapped on tight (but not too tight) to give them even stronger input.

Invest in 8–10 cloth bags of rice (in 3 lb. or 5 lb. bags). Have the child move and stack these bags several times a day in different designated places in or near the classroom.

Below are a few more general suggestions to address how to keep a child motivated and engaged.

1. Look closely at the toys you have available for your students to play with. If certain toys are not used then get rid of them and try to replace them with something new and more stimulating. Kids love toys made of real materials such as wood (rather than weightless colored toys). In a large school with numerous classrooms it is a good idea for all the classroom teachers to have a toy swap. Bringing in another classroom's toys is like getting new toys.

2. The same is true for books. It's not uncommon for the same books to occupy the same classroom for the entire year without any additions or deletions. Kids need to be exposed to new books that come recommended, either by other teachers or on internet sites that rate children's books. If your school can't afford new books then perhaps someone will be daring enough to take out a few books from their public library and keep track of when they need to be returned.

3. Story Time: Decide on which book you are going to read to your class the day before. Scan it and look for any places where children can help act out parts, perhaps even giving them simple props. The more kids you can involve, the more likely they are to have their attention focused on the story. Obviously you can't do this by just picking a book off the shelf.

4. Guided play: A great many classrooms will schedule free play or Centers as opportunities for the children to play with different toys or materials, and of course with other students. Teachers don't always have the luxury of sitting among a small group of children who are building with blocks or playing in the kitchen. But there is certainly enough time to give them the idea of an imaginative scenario that the kids can then act out. For example, children who request to play in the toy kitchen area can be told that they are going to a restaurant to eat. Someone can be the mom, dad, or child, and someone else can be the cook or the waiter. Or perhaps they can be going to the grocery store. Perhaps there are costumes or clothing props to make this more inviting. Look in on them to give them additional ideas to direct their play. Unfortunately many young children still do not have these basic imagination skills. Guide them with your ideas.

5. Think of it... Imaginary play almost always involves a person or an animal—a living thing. Make sure that you have toy characters and additional props that can be integrated into their play. How often I have heard that a child merely lines up trains or cars and pushes them back and forth. By introducing scale-size people, then some are passengers, conductors, or pedestrians, and more imaginary play is possible. Once again, you may need to explain who these characters are supposed to be, and perhaps what story they are acting out.

INDEX

Attention Deficit Disorder (ADD)
  and sensory seekers 46–7
auditory issues
  and sensory averse child 82
Autism Spectrum Disorder (ASD)
  diagnosis of 128–9

behavioral observations
  for sensory averse child 88–90,
    97–8, 106–7
  for sensory indulgent child 118
  for sensory seekers 51–4, 63–4
  for sensory sensitivity 73–5
  for under-responsive child 36–8
bloodstream 12
bodily functions
  description of 11–12
body awareness
  and behavioral responses
    48–50
books
  in pre–school classroom 153
brain
  function of 12–13
  and self-regulation response
    20–1
  and sensory system 14–15, 19

cutting difficulties 142–3

Diagnostic and Statistical
  Manual of Mental Disorders
  (DSM) 128
digestive organs 11

fine motor skills
  in pre–school classroom 138–43
  for sensory averse child 90–1,
    98–100, 108–10
  for sensory indulgent child
    119–20
  for sensory seekers 55–7, 65–6
  for sensory sensitivity 75–6
  for under-responsive child
    39–40

gross motor skills
  for sensory averse child 98,
    107–8
  for sensory seekers 54–5
guided play
  in pre–school classroom 153–4

high sensory thresholds
  achieving 25
  and behavioral responses 26–33
  and body awareness 49
  response to pain 31–2

imaginary play
  in pre–school classroom 154
Infant Toddler Sensory Profile
  and sensory averse child 92–4,
    101–3

low sensory thresholds
  achieving 25–6
  behavioral responses of 69–70
  and sensory sensitivity 70–2

medical history
  for sensory averse child 88,
    96–7, 105–6
  for sensory indulgent child
    115–18
  for sensory seekers 51, 62–3
  for sensory sensitivity 73
  for under-responsive child 36

neuromotor assessments
  for sensory averse child 98,
    107–8
  for sensory seekers 54–5

occupational therapy
  evaluations
  of sensory averse child 87–113
  of sensory indulgent child
    114–23
  of sensory seekers 50–61
  of sensory sensitivity 72–9
  of under-responsive child 35–43
oral issues
  and sensory averse child 83–4

pain
  in high sensory thresholds 31–2
Peabody Development Motor
  Scales
  for sensory averse child 90–1,
    98–101, 108–10
  for sensory indulgent child
    118–20
  for sensory seekers 55–7, 64–8
  for sensory sensitivity 75–9
  for under-responsive child
    38–43
pre-school classroom
  books in 153
  cutting difficulties 142–3
  fine motor skills in 138–43
  group activities in 145–6
  guided play in 153–4
  imaginary play in 154
  movement in 151–2

occupational therapist
  interventions in 137–8
poor registration children in
  143
sensory averse children in
  144–5
sensory seekers in 143–4, 147–51
sensory sensitivity in 144
story time in 153
suggestions for 152–4
toys in 152–3
writing problems 138–42
poor registration children
  behavioral responses of 26–33
  in pre–school classroom 143
  response to pain 31–2
proprioceptive system
  description of 17–19
  for under-responsive child 42

referrals
  for sensory averse child 87,
    95–6, 104–5
  for sensory indulgent child 114
  for sensory seekers 50–1, 62
  for sensory sensitivity 72
  for under-responsive child 35
respiratory system 11–12

self-regulation response 20–1,
  123–6
sensory averse child
  auditory issues 82
  behavioral observations 88–90,
    97–8, 106–7
  behavioral responses of 80–6
  fine motor skills 90–1, 98–100,
    108–10
  gross motor skills 98, 107–8
  Infant Toddler Sensory Profile
    92–4, 101–3
  medical history 88, 96–7, 105–6
  neuromotor assessments 98,
    107–8

occupational therapy
evaluations 87–113
oral issues 83–4
Peabody Developmental Motor
Scales 90–1, 98–101, 108–10
in pre-school classroom 144–5
referrals for 87, 95–6, 104–5
sensory integration 91–2, 100–1,
110–13
site for evaluation 87–8, 96, 105
tactile issues 85–6
visual issues 82–3
sensory developmental stages
131–4
sensory indulgent child
behavioral observations 118
fine motor skills 119–20
medical history 115–18
occupational therapy
evaluations 114–23
Peabody Developmental Motor
Scales 118–20
referrals for 114
sensory integration 120–2
site for evaluation 115
sensory integration
for sensory averse child 91–2,
100–1, 110–13
for sensory indulgent child
120–2
for sensory seekers 57–61, 66–8
for sensory sensitivity 76–9
for under-responsive child
40–3
Sensory Processing Disorder
(SPD)
developmental stages of 131–4
diagnosis of 127–30
sensory seekers
and Attention Deficit Disorder
46–7
behavioral observations 51–4,
63–4
behavioral responses of 44–8

fine motor skills 55–7, 65–6
gross motor skills 54–5
medical history 51, 62–3
neuromotor assessments 54–5
occupational therapy
evaluations 50–61
Peabody Development Motor
Scales 55–7, 64–8
in pre-school classroom 143–4,
147–51
referrals for 50–1, 62
sensory integration 57–61, 66–8
site for evaluation 51, 62
sensory sensitivity
behavioral observations 73–5
fine motor skills 75–6
and low sensory thresholds
70–2
medical history 73
occupational therapy
evaluation 72–9
Peabody Development Motor
Scales 75–9
in pre-school classroom 144
referrals for 72
sensory integration 76–9
site for evaluation 73
sensory system
and brain 14–15, 19
as continuum 20–1
importance of 13–15
individual differences 22–3
and proprioceptive system
17–19
and self-regulation response
20–1
and vestibular system 16–17
workings of 15–16, 19
sensory thresholds
description of 24–5
high sensory thresholds 25,
26–33
low sensory thresholds 25–6
tipping points in 25

site for evaluation
  for sensory averse child 87–8,
    96, 105
  for sensory indulgent child 115
  for sensory seekers 51, 62
  for sensory sensitivity 73
  for under-responsive child 35–6
story time
  in pre–school classroom 153

tactile issues
  and sensory averse child 85–6
tipping points
  in sensory thresholds 25
toys
  in pre–school classroom 152–3

under-responsive children
  behavioral observations 36–8
  behavioral responses of 33–4

fine motor skills 40–1
medical history 36
occupational therapy
  evaluation of 35–43
Peabody Development Motor
  Scales 38–43
referrals for 35
sensory integration 40–3
site for evaluation 35–6

vestibular system
  description of 16–17
  and sensory adverse child 84–5
  for under-responsive child 41–2
visual issues
  and sensory averse child 82–3

waste management system 12
writing problems 138–42